The Hāthīgumphā Inscription of Khāravela and The Bhabru Edict of Aśoka

The Hāthīgumphā Inscription of Khāravela and The Bhabru Edict of Aśoka

— A Critical Study —

Shashi Kant

D.K.Printworld(P)Ltd.
NEW DELHI - 110 015

Cataloging in Publication Data — DK

Shashi Kant, 1932 –
The Hāthīgumphā inscription of Khāravela and the Bhabru Edict of Aśoka.
Includes bibliographical references (p.).
Includes index.

1. India — History — 324 BC — 1000 AD — Sources. 2. Khāravela, King of Kalinga. 3. Aśoka, King of Magadha, fl. 272 BC — 232 BC 4. Inscriptions, Prakrit. 5. Buddhism — India — History — Sources. I. Title.

First Edition 1971
Second Revised Edition 2000

ISBN 81-246-0139-9

Published and printed by:
D.K. Printworld (P) Ltd.
Regd. office : '*Sri Kunj*', F-52, Bali Nagar
New Delhi-110015
Phones : (011) 545-3975, 546-6019; *Fax* : (011) 546-5926
E-mail: dkprint@4mis.com

To those
who are interested
in digging up
the past

Foreword

The *Hāthīgumphā Inscription of Khāravela* is one of the few significant sources available for the dark period in the history of India between the fall of the Mauryan dynasty and the rise of the Guptas. Composed as it is in a very obscure Prakrit, and its characters badly weathered by centuries of exposure to the elements and in places quite illegible, this inscription has long been the subject of a great controversy among historians and palaeographers. Many uncertainties and ambiguities still remain. The date of the inscription is as yet not finally settled, and opinions vary over a period of about two hundred years. Certain scholars believe that it is a little later than the inscriptions of Aśoka, while others would date it not long before the beginning of the Christian era.

The new edition and translation of this inscription by Dr. Shashi Kant marks a great step in our understanding of this very difficult historical document. In many particulars the fresh interpretation presented here is an obvious improvement over those of previous students of the subject. After reading Dr. Kant's typescript, I find myself in agreement with him in most particulars, though I must record my doubts as to his views on the chronology of the inscription. The style of the script suggests to me a date in the first century BC, and I would prefer to interpret the obscure chronological data in the inscription itself as referring to a period 300 years after the Nanda King, and not 103. But authorities may differ, and in general I would heartily recommend this interpretation to all students of Indian history.

With this is included a further study of one of Aśoka's most obscure inscriptions, the Bhabru Edict. This little document is as important for the history of Buddhism as the Khāravela's Hāthīgumphā Inscription is for that of Jainism, and it arouses many questions as to the correct interpretation of the passages of scripture referred to and the relations of church and state under Aśoka's regime. Here, too, Dr. Shashi Kant has produced new theories of great importance and I recommend them to all students of Indian history and religions.

January, 1971

A.L. Basham
Ph. D., D.Litt.
Professor of Oriental Civilisation
The Australian National University
Canberra (Australia)

Preface to the Second Edition

It is indeed gratifying that the book has attracted notice of reputed scholars in the field. It has been extensively reviewed both in India and outside. It has also found a place in the curriculum of several universities. The compliments of Prof. Jes P. Asmussen that it is a fine piece of work, of Prof. A.L. Basham that he found it a very impressive study, of Prof. N.S. Ramaswami that it is a lucidly argued and fairly presented attempt to set out the problems and to find the answers, of Dr. Krishna Deva that the book is indeed very well written and documented, and of Dr. Mahesh Kumar Sharan that the book for the first time tackles some of the very complicated problems of Indian history from every conceivable angle, as well as the appreciation by the learned reviewers, are highly encouraging. I am grateful to all these savants for having bestowed so much thought on my book and for making some valuable suggestions, as also the editors and publishers of the Journals for sparing space for the reviews.

To make the work more useful, I have added further annotations, as also Section III on the genesis of the Prakrit languages and the ancient Indian scripts. Some controversial issues, *e.g.*, the *Himavanta-Therāvalī*, the era of dates given by Khāravela, the dates of the Buddha's *parinirvāṇa* and Mahāvīra's *nirvāṇa*, identification of Asikanagara and Kaṁhabeṁnā, interpretation of *coyaṭha*, and problems relating to Sātakaṁni and Bahasatimita, Kaliṅga Jina, Schism and Khāravela, the Schism, Kaliṅga and Jainism, Nandas and Jainism, and Aśoka and Kaliṅga, have been discussed in Appendix III. The bibliography has been updated.

In orthography, textual words and ancient names have been rendered into the Roman script with appropriate diacritical marks; the place names have been spelt as in *The Oxford School Atlas* (29th edn., 1997). Locations have been updated according to current geography.

The photo-plates of the Hāthīgumphā Inscription are being published by courtesy of the Patna Museum, Patna, that of the Bhabru Edict by courtesy of the Asiatic Society of Bengal, Calcutta, and the other photographs by courtesy of the Archaeological Survey of India.

It would be ungrateful of me if I fail to put on record now that the insight to probe into the mysteries of epigraphy is a byproduct of the method of teaching Epigraphy by the late Prof. C.D. Chatterji of Lucknow University. And it would be callous on my part if I do not mention my wife Manjari who bears with me to let me burn night-light in the rough-and-tough of my literary, journalistic and research pursuits

I am thankful to Mr. Susheel K. Mittal, Director, D.K. Printworld (P) Ltd., for bringing out the second revised edition.

Jyoti Nikunj, Charbagh
Lucknow - 226004

Nov. 7, 1999 **Shashi Kant**

Preface to the First Edition

THE Hāthīgumphā Inscription is the only extant record about a forgotten epoch in Indian history. It is highly personal and that makes it all the more important for the history of its author. It is unique inasmuch as it gives the dates of earlier events, records the doings of its author in a chronological sequence regnal yearwise, and presents the earliest written exposition of Jain terminology and corroboration of the Jain scriptural tradition.

The Bhabru Edict is earlier in date. It is also personal in character. The significant thing about this epigraph is that it provides the earliest written record of the Buddhist scripture and monastic organisation.

The studies of these inscriptions, presented here, are independent but they have been combined as they have thematic similarity. Their interpretations suffered in the past for want of correct appreciation of the Jain and Buddhist traditions. Fresh attempt has been made here to read these inscriptions keeping in view the tenor and context, and to correlate and interpret the data with reference to relevant traditions and more recent archaeological finds.

For the studies presented here I owe a debt of deep gratitude to all those savants whose patient researches enabled me to know something of our heritage. A great many of them are no longer with us, but the fruits of their toil inspire us and sustain us in the uphill task of exploring new data and appraising the known data so that the missing links in our history may be found and the coming generations may be better informed about their history and culture.

Prof. A. L. Basham, Prof. R.K. Dikshit and Prof. K.D. Bajpai have been kind enough to go through the typescript and I am thankful to them for their appreciation. These studies would not haye taken a shape but for the encouragement I received from my father Dr. Jyoti Prasad Jain. The credit for getting it into print goes to the Prints India.

Lucknow **Shashi Kant**

December, 1971

Contents

Critique

The empire of Khāravela was short-lived, but he evidently was as important for the history of Jainism as Aśoka was for that of Buddhism. The documents most important for the history of religion are the object of Dr. Kant's penetrating study. His book certainly marks a great step in our understanding of these difficult historical texts, a fact sharply stressed by the careful text edition, the sound translation and the illuminating remarks on Jainism, Buddhism and Aśoka, and the personal history of Khāravela.

PROF. JES P. ASMUSSEN
University of Copenhagen, Denmark
(*Acta Orientalia*, XXXVI)

Dr. Kant sums up the earlier research and gives his own translation with copious notes on other authors' views. His work gives many original suggestions.

PROF. J. VACEK
Academia Praha,
Czechoslovakia
(*Archiv Orientalini*, XLII)

Dr. Shashi Kant's monograph is useful in understanding not only the problems, but also because of the light it throws on the brilliant career of its author, Khāravela. It will be of much help to the students of ancient Indian culture because of the various readings of both the records which have been given by the author together with a comparative palaeographical chart and an exhaustive bibliography.

Dr. M.K. Dhavalikar
Deccan College, Pune
(*Annals of the Bhandarkar Oriental Research Institute*, LIII)

An account of the socio-political conditions in Khāravela's time, describing fairs and festivals, polygamy, four-fold army, navy and political alliances or confederacies has been carefully incorporated. Two maps showing (1) the extent of Khāravela's empire and his wide military expeditions and (2) Aśoka Maurya's empire, and a bibliography have added no doubt to the value of the book.

Dr. B.K. Majumdar
Calcutta University
(*Quarterly Review of Historical Studies*, IX, 4)

Patient and diligent decipherment and intelligent interpretation of a controversial record, may reveal the past in newer and newer perspectives. Dr. Shashi Kant's book under review is an example thereof. His present study of the epigraph helps understanding this very difficult historical document better than before. A fresh meaning and interpretation of the Bhabru edict, based on relevant Buddhist traditions, is also thought provoking.

Dr. Devendra Handa
Punjab University, Chandigarh
(*Vishveshvaranand Indological Journal*, X)

Reproduction of original epigraphs and the palaeographic chart have greatly enhanced the usefulness of the work.

PROF. M.C. CHOUDHURY
Kurukshetra University
(*Prācī-Jyoti*, VIII)

The book, written in lucid and simple style, is a very useful and helpful contribution to the literature on the subject.

DR. M.L. SHARMA
Jaipur
(*Journal of the Rajasthan Institute of Historical Research*, IX, 3)

Dr. Shashi Kant's monograph is a lucidly argued and fairly presented attempt to set out the problems and to find the answers. Nothing is more probable than that Khāravela, a pious Jaina, should have dated the events in his epigraph in the Mahāvīra Era which it is believed, began on the day of the *nirvāṇa* of Mahāvīra, October 15, 527 BC.

The Tamil Sangam poems refer to the Nandas. There is an old tradition of the south's contacts with them, though these might be less intense than those with their successors, the Mauryas, of whom Bindusāra is said to have invaded the region.

The Hāthīgumphā epigraph is also important in Jaina theological history. Dr. Shashi Kant seems to break new ground in explaining its significance.

The Bhabru edict mentions many Buddhist scriptures, the identification of which has caused some difficulties. Dr. Shashi Kant suggests many identifications of the sacred texts mentioned in his immaculate edition of the edict.

This book provides much of the critical apparatus needed for each scholar to judge for himself. Dr. Shashi Kant brings to his task a profound knowledge of Jaina and Buddhist religions, the keen sense of the epigraphical scholar, and a willingness to accept the latest archaeological findings.

PROF. N.S. RAMASWAMI
Madras University
(*Journal of Oriental Research*,
XXXVIII, Pt. I-IV)

Although one may not agree with all that Dr. Shashi Kant says about the chronology of Khāravela, his interpretation of the unique record is highly critical, refreshing and sparkles with originality and his reconstruction of the social, cultural and religious life from the data furnished by the epigraphy is indeed brilliant. His interpretation of the Bhabru Edict of Aśoka also breaks new ground and provides a scintillating approach to a difficult and knotty epigraph. The book is indeed very well written and documented and marks a valuable contribution to Indological studies.

DR. KRISHNA DEVA
Archaeological Survey of India
(*Purātattva*, No. 6)

The new edition and translation of the *Hāthīgumphā Inscription of Khāravela* by Dr. Shashi Kant marks a great step forward in our understanding of this very difficult historical document. In many particulars the fresh interpretation presented here is an obvious improvement over those of previous students of the subject.

The Bhabru Edict of Aśoka is as important for the history

of Buddhism as the Khāravela's Hāthīgumphā Inscription is for that of Jainism and it arouses many questions as to the correct interpretation of the passages of scripture referred to and the relations of church and state under Aśoka's regime. Here, too, Dr. Shashi Kant has produced new theories of great importance.

DR. A.L. BASHAM
The Australian National
University, Canberra

Dr. Shashi Kant has made an unbiased study of the two important inscriptions. His approach is new and critical.

DR. RAM KUMAR DIKSHIT
Lucknow University

Dr. Shashi Kant has studied these two important inscriptions critically. The book will go a long way in dispelling several wrong conceptions pertaining to the subject.

PROF. KRISHNA DUTT BAJPAI
Dr. H.S. Gaur University, Sagar

The approach is scholarly but Dr. Shashi Kant's deep understanding of the subject has made the contents intelligible even to the average reader.

DR. GANGA RAM GARG
Gurukul Kangri Vishvavidyalaya,
Haridwar

No better book has come to light so far on the subject.

ITIHĀSA-MANĪṢĪ DR. JYOTI PRASAD JAIN
Eminent Jainologist

The book for the first time tackles some of the very complicated problems of Indian history from every conceivable angle, and will serve as a guideline both for the post-graduate scholars and the advanced researchers in the field.

DR. MAHESH KUMAR SHARAN
Magadh University, Bodh Gaya

Your book is a marvellous work, many a times giving new readings and fresh interpretations.

DR. M.D. VASANTHARAJ
Mysore University

Abbreviations

A.B.O.R.I.	:	*Annals of the Bhandarkar Oriental Research Institute*
A.S.I.	:	Archaeological Survey of India
AD	:	Christian Era
App.	:	Appendix
B	:	Dr. B.M. Barua in *I.H.Q.*, XIV
BC	:	Before Christ
cr.	:	*circa*
cf.	:	compare
Cunn.	:	Sir Alexander Cunningham
e.g.	:	for example
ed.	:	editor
edn.	:	edition
E.I.	:	*Epigraphia Indica*
ff	:	and the following
fn.	:	footnote
I.A.	:	*Indian Antiquary*
I.A.R.	:	*Indian Archaeology — A Review*
i.e.	:	that is
I.H.Q.	:	*Indian Historical Quarterly*
ibid.	:	the same
Intro.	:	Introduction
J	:	K.P. Jayaswal & R.D. Banerji in *E.I.*, XX
J.B.O.R.S.	:	*Journal of Bihar and Orissa Research Society*

J.D.L.	:	*Journal of the Deptt. of Letters*
J.O.R.	:	*Journal of the Oriental Research*
J.R.A.S.	:	*Journal of the Royal Asiatic Society*
J.U.P.H.S.	:	*Journal of the U.P. Historical Society*
K.R.E.	:	Kaliṅga Rock Edict
L	:	Line
lit.	:	literally
M.A.S.B.	:	*Memoirs of the Asiatic Society of Bengal*
M.E.	:	Mahāvīra Era
M.P.E.	:	Minor Pillar Edict
M.R.E.	:	Minor Rock Edict
op. cit.	:	The work cited
opp.	:	opposite
p./pp.	:	page/pages
pl.	:	plate
pt.	:	part
R.	:	River
R.E.	:	Rock Edict
ref.	:	reference
S	:	D.C. Sircar in *S.I.*
S.B.E.	:	*Sacred Books of the East*
S.I.	:	*Select Inscriptions* by D.C. Sircar
sec.	:	section
Skt.	:	Sanskrit
tr., trans.	:	translation, translator
v.	:	verse
vide	:	see
viz.	:	namely
vol.	:	Volume

Transliteration Chart

a	ā	i	ī	u	ū	e	ai	o	au
अ	आ	इ	ई	उ	ऊ	ए	ऐ	ओ	औ
	ा	ि	ी	ु	ू	े	ै	ो	ौ

ṁ	ḥ	ṛ
अं	अः	ऋ
	ः	ृ

k	kh	g	gh	ṅ
क्	ख्	ग्	घ्	ङ्
c	ch	j	jh	ñ
च्	छ्	ज्	झ्	ञ्
ṭ	ṭh	ḍ	ḍh	ṇ
ट्	ठ्	ड्	ढ्	ण्
t	th	d	dh	n
त्	थ्	द्	ध्	न्
p	ph	b	bh	m
प्	फ्	ब्	भ्	म्

y	r	l	v
य्	र्	ल्	व्
ś	ṣ	s	h
श्	ष्	स्	ह्

ks	tr	jñ	ḷ
क्ष्	त्र्	ज्ञ्	ळ्

List of Plates

1

The Inscription

Introductory

THE Hāthīgumphā Inscription of Mahāmeghavāhana Khāravela has had a fascinating course since its discovery in AD 1825. It is not a royal panegyric merely; it is an epitome of history. Such chronological narration of events in a matter-of-fact manner is yet to be found on rock, pillar or stone of an ancient date. It has an order and a sequence not met so far in any other inscription of comparable date and that makes it much more valuable as a historical document. Moreover, it forms the only source of information about its author and subject.

The inscriptions of Devānāṁpriya Priyadarśi Aśoka, definitely earlier than this epigraph of Khāravela, give very little information of political nature and read more like sermons incised on stone. More or less contemporary Nanaghat Inscription and the later Nasik Cave Inscriptions of the Sātavāhanas, as also the Girnar Inscription of Rudradāman, present little as a chronological record. They, as well as the later *praśasti*s, or eulogistic inscriptions, as they are so aptly called, generally seem to make vague claims and assertions for their royal authors or patrons through praiseful epithets.

In fact, such a historically potent epigraph is yet to be discovered elsewhere in the contemporary world. In India, the place which is assigned to Kalhaṇa's *Rājataraṅgiṇī* among ancient historical writings, is well deserved by this inscription in the realm of epigraphy and it betrays well-informed historical consciousness among the Indians more than two thousand years ago.

To use the terminology of Kauṭilya, it is a *Prajñāpana Lekha* (Public Notification) engraved for the purpose of narrating (*ākhyānam*) the principal events of the life and reign of King Khāravela, and is endowed with all the six qualities of *artha-krama* (proper arrangement), *sambandha* (relevancy), *paripūrṇatā* (completeness), *mādhuryam* (sweetness), *audāryam* (dignity) and *spaṣṭatvam* (lucidity), that make a good composition.[1]

Decipherment

No wonder therefore that this inscription has been engaging the attention of the Indologists and claiming their best labours for the last nearly one-and-a-half century. The story of its decipherment is on that account no less fascinating. It was first noticed by Stirling in AD 1825 who gave an account of it in the *Asiatic Researches,* XV (pp. 313ff.), and was first published by Prinsep from an eye-copy prepared by Kittoe in 1837, in the *Journal of the Asiatic Society of Bengal*, VI (pp. 1075-91, plate LVIII). A tracing of the inscription was published by Cunningham in the *Corpus Inscriptionum Indicarum*, I (pl. XVIII, pp. 27f, 98-101, 132ff.), in 1877, and a version of it, by Raja Rajendra Lala Mitra in the *Antiquities of Orissa*, II (pp. 16 ff.), in 1880. The same year a cast was also taken to the Indian Museum, Calcutta.

It was, however, only in 1885 that the first reliable version was given by Dr. Bhagwan Lal Indraji in the *Actes du Sixième Congrès International des Orientalistes* (pt. III, sec. 2, pp. 152-77). He also made out the name as *Khāravela*. Bühler suggested certain corrections in 1895 and 1898.[2] The first inked impression was taken in 1906 by Dr. T. Bloch and was sent to Prof. Keilhorn

1. *Arthaśāstra*, X (trans. R. Shamasastry, fourth edn., pp. 71-75).
2. 'Origin of Indian Brāhmī Alphabet', *Indian Studies*, No. III, p. 13.

who passed it on to Dr. J.F. Fleet. In 1910 Fleet published certain corrections in Line 16[1] and Lüders also published a summary.[2] In 1913 Prof. R.D. Banerji examined certain portions and in 1917 two inked impressions were again taken, one of which was published in the *Journal of Bihar and Orissa Research Society*, III, 4 (pl. I), and the other was sent to Dr. F.W. Thomas. Dr. K.P. Jayaswal discussed and read it on the basis of that impression in *J.B.O.R.S.*, III, 4 (pp. 425ff.),[3] and the next year he published a revised text of his reading after checking it from the rock itself.[4] In 1919 Jayaswal and Banerji examined the inscription on the spot and H. Panday of the Archaeological Survey Department prepared a cast of which two paper impressions were also taken. "It is as successful a copy as the present condition of the original allowed it to be." It was published in 1927 in *J.B.O.R.S.*, XIII. The cast and the paper impressions are preserved in the Patna Museum. In 1924, Jayaswal and Banerji went over the corrections and in 1927 and 1928 the former published the results of his further studies.[5] In 1929 Dr. B.M. Barua also edited this inscription at No. 1 in his *Old Brāhmī Inscriptions in the Udayagiri and Khaṇḍagiri Caves*. Sten Konow,[6] Thomas,[7] Muni Jina Vijaya[8] and R.P. Chanda[9] also added some useful information.

A somewhat definitive stage in decipherment was marked by a fuller discussion of its palaeography by Banerji in the *Memoirs of the Asiatic Society of Bengal*, X (pp. 133ff.), as also

---

1. *J.R.A.S*, 1910, pp. 242ff, 824ff.
2. *E.I.*, X, App., pp. 160-61 (No. 1345).
3. Banerji's Note is on pp. 486ff. therein.
4. *J.B.O.R.S.*, IV, pp. 364ff.
5. *J.B.O.R.S.*, XIII, pp. 221ff. ; XIV, pp. 150ff.
6. *Acta Orientalia*, I, pp. 12ff.
7. *J.R.A.S.*, 1922, pp. 83-84.
8. Quoted in *E.I.*, XX; also his letter in *Anekānta*, I, 6-7, p. 351.
9. *I.H.Q.*, 1929, p. 395f., 595.

by a joint edition of the text by Jayaswal and Banerji in 1929-30 in the *Epigraphia Indica*, XX (pp. 71-89, No. 7). The latter also on that basis reconstructed the history of Khāravela in his *History of Orissa*, I (pp. 71-92). Barua did not agree with them and so he published his revised edition in 1938 in the *Indian Historical Quarterly*, XIV, 3 (pp. 459-85). In 1942 Dr. D.C. Sircar published his readings and annotations in the *Select Inscriptions*, I (pp. 206-13, No. 91).[1] Perhaps no other single epigraph has been the subject of so much research and controversy. And yet it leaves much to be desired.

Site

Some three miles to the north and north-east of Bhubaneshwar in the Puri district of Orissa is situated a low range of hills called the Khaṇḍagiri and Udayagiri. These hills preserve some of the early specimens of rock-cut architecture in eastern India. The excavations are known in the local parlance as the *gumphā*, or cave. The two-storeyed Rāṇī Gumphā on the Udayagiri represents the Orissan rock-cut cave architecture at its best.[2] To the west of it is the Baḍā Hāthīgumphā (Big Elephant Cave),[3] "a natural cavern, very little improved and enlarged by art", on the southern face of the Udayagiri.

On the overhanging brow of this Hāthīgumphā is engraved the precious record of the doings of King Khāravela of Kaliṅga,

1. Among further notable contributions may be added : Sircar in *The History and Culture of the Indian People*, II, pp. 211ff; Balchandra Jain's *Kaliṅga-Cakravarti* (in Hindi); Dr. N.K. Sahu's *Khāravela*, and also in *A History of Orissa*, pp. 327-30; Jagannath in *A Comprehensive History of India*, II, pp. 111-15; Dr. L.N. Sahu — *Uḍīsā mein Jaina Dharma* (Hindi tr.), pp. 39-73; and Dr. J.P. Jain — *Bhāratīya Itihāsa: Eka Dṛṣṭi* (in Hindi), pp. 180-90.

2. For fuller account, see Percy Brown — *Indian Architecture* (*Buddhist and Hindu Periods*), (fourth edn., 1959), pp. 28-30.

3. There are two Hāthīgumphās on the same hill. To distinguish between the two, one is called Choṭā (Small) Hāthīgumphā and the other, merely Hāthīgumphā or Baḍā (Big) Hāthīgumphā.

otherwise little known to history, in seventeen lines covering an area 15 feet 1 inch in length and 5 feet 6 inches in height. "The inscription begins on the southern face and is continued up to a place where the stone has actually become the roof of the cave. The last eight or nine lines occur on a sloping surface where it is difficult either to read or copy them. Below the inscription the walls of the natural cavern have been chiselled straight and at places are as beautifully polished as those of the Barabar caves. Near the floor there are sundry rock-cut partitions which do not appear to have been regular walls as they do not go up to the roof. In the dressed and polished portion of the side or the wall of the cave there are a number of later inscriptions (of about the tenth or eleventh century AD)[1] many of which contain proper names which are not of any historical interest. They prove, however, that the cave was visited by pilgrims up to the tenth century AD and therefore it must have been considered some sort of a sacred shrine. The bed of the cave is full of sand in front and unless it is excavated its original form cannot be determined. The Hāthīgumphā stands at right angles to Svargapurī and Mañcapurī on its left and the Sarpa cave on its right. There are several small and large excavations on the top of the boulder which forms the roof of the cave."[2]

Although the entire record appears to have been very carefully inscribed, it has suffered greatly from Nature's fury. The record as it is now, is very much weather-beaten and shows signs of progressive natural decay. Three main problems confronting the epigraphists in deciphering it are: firstly, the different forms of a few letters, secondly, the misleading chisel-marks, and thirdly, the changes wrought by natural decay and weather conditions. As early as 1917 it was observed that "the rock was roughly dressed on the right-hand side. The chisel-marks of the dressing are misleading; they tend to produce

---

1. See, *Annual Report of Achaeological Survey of India*, 1922-23, p. 130.
2. Jayaswal and Banerji (*E.I.*, XX, p. 72).

misreadings. These long and irregular marks left by the original dressing, are not the only pitfalls. Rain-water which trickles down the roof of the cave has cut into the letters and produced a few letter-like marks. Natural decay produced by time has given misleading turns to numerous letters. Even hornets like to take liberty with the record of the Emperor Khāravela with perfect impunity and have added a few irregular marks on it."[1]

On the basis of the plates published in *J.B.O.R.S.*, III and XIII, and *I.H.Q.*, XIV,[2] the inscription may be read as follows. Variants as well as my reasons for accepting a particular reading or restoration are given in the notes below. Punctuation marks have been indicated within brackets. The particles and characters which are not quite distinct but are most probably there, have also been shown within brackets. Components of compound words have been separated by hyphens where feasible.

Text

Line 1 Namo Arahaṁtānaṁ[3] (.) Namo sava-Sidhānaṁ (..)

---

1. *J.B.O.R.S.*, III, 4, p. 430.
2. B.V. Nath, Superintendent of Archaeology and Museums, Orissa, had informed that an inpression was also taken by Dr. B. Ch. Chhabra in 1954. It has not been published. It may also be added that due to the progressive decay of the original the later impressions are likely to miss some characters, hence not much help can be derived from them.

   (Below, J stands for Jayaswal and Banerji in *E.I.*, B for Barua in *I.H.Q.*, and S for Sircar in *S.I.*)
3. J — Ar(i)haṁtānaṁ

   B — Araha(ṁ)tānaṁ

   Since the medial *i* is doubtful, it would be better to read *Arahaṁtānaṁ*.

Airena[1] Mahārājena Mahāmeghavāhanena[2] Cetirājava(ṁ)sa-vadhanena[3] Pasatha-subha-lakhanena[4] Caturaṁta-luṭhaṇa-guṇa-upetena[5] Kaliṁgādhipatinā-Siri-Khāravelena

Line 2 paṁdarasa-vasāni siri-kaḍāra-sarīra-vatā kīḍitā Kumāra-kīḍikā (.) Tato Lekha-rūpā-gaṇanā-vavahāra-vidhi-visāradena Sava-vijāvadātena nava-vasāni Yovaraja(ṁ) pasāsitaṁ[6] (.) Saṁpuṇa-catuvīsati-vaso tadāni vadhamāna-sesa-yovanābhivijayo[7] tatiye —

Line 3 Kaliṁga-rājavaṁse-purisayuge Mahārājābhisecanaṁ[8]

---

1. J & B — Airena

   S — Aireṇa

   Since throughout the inscription *na*, and not *ṇa*, has been used in the third case, it should be *Airena*.

2. J & B — Māhāmeghavāhanena

   S — Mahāmeghavāhanena

3. J — vasa

   B — va(ṁ)sa

   Vasa gives no sense here as it has been used in the meaning of 'year' throughout the inscription.

4. J — lakhanena

   B — lakha(ṇ)ena

5. J — luṭhita-guṇ-opahitena

   B — luṭhana-guṇa-upetena

   S — Luṭha(ṇa)-guṇa-upitena

   Chanda was the first to make out *guṇa-upetena* correctly.

6. J — pasāsitaṁ

   B — va sāsitaṁ, *or*, pasāsitaṁ

   Va sāsitaṁ gives no meaning.

7. J — vadhamāna-sesayo Ven-ābhivijayo

   B — vadha(māna) (sesa)yovanābhivijayo

   S — vadhamānasesayovenābhivijayo

8. J — Māhārajābhisecanaṁ

   B — Mahārājābhisecanaṁ

pāpunāti (.) Abhisitamato ca padhame vase vāta-vihata[1] gopura-pākāra-nivesanaṁ paṭisaṁkhārayati Kaliṁganagari-Khibīraṁ[2] sitala[3]-taḍāga-pāḍiyo ca baṁdhāpayati savūyāna-paṭisaṁthapanaṁ ca

Line 4 kārayati panatīsāhi-sata-sahasehi (,) pakatiyo ca raṁjayati (.) Dutiye ca vase acitayitā Sātakaṁniṁ[4] pacima-disaṁ haya-gaja-nara-radha-bahulaṁ-daṁḍaṁ paṭhāpayati[5] Kaṁhabeṁnā[6]-gatāya ca senāya vitāsiti[7] Asika-nagaraṁ[8] (.) Tatiye puna vase

Line 5 Gaṁdhava-veda-budho dapa-nata-gīta-vādita-saṁdaṁsanāhi[9] usava-samāja-kārāpanāhi ca

---

1. J — vāta-vihita —
   B — vāta-vihata —
2. J — Kaliṁga-nagari-Khibīra —
   B — Kaliṁga-nagari-Khi(b)īra(ṁ), *or*, Khi(p)īra(ṁ), (,)
   S — Kaliṁganagari Khibī(raṁ)
3. J — isi-tāla —
   B — sitala —
4. J — Sātakaṁniṁ
   B — Sātakaṇiṁ
5. J — paṭhāpayati
   B — pathāpayati
6. J — Kañha-beṁnā —
   B — Kanhabeṁnaṁ
7. J — vitāsitaṁ
   B — vitāsiti
   The context also warrants a finite verb.
8. J — M(u)sika-nagaraṁ
   B — Asikanagaraṁ
   The character is more clearly *a* than *mu*.
9. J — saṁdaṁsanāhi
   B — saṁdasanāhi

kīḍapayati[1] nagariṁ (.) Tathā cavuthe vase Vijādharādhivāsaṁ ahata-puva-Kaliṁga-puvarāja n(i)v(e)s(i)t(i)[2] — vitadha-makuṭa-sabila(dhi)te[3] ca[4] nikhita-chata-

Line 6 bhiṁgāre hita-ratana-sāpateye sava-Raṭhika-Bhojake pāde vaṁdāpayati (.) Paṁcame ca dānī[5] vase Naṁdarāja-tivasasata-oghāṭitaṁ Tanasuliyavāṭā-

---

1. J — ca kīḍapayati

   B — kīḍāpayati

   Ca is also necessary to connect the two *pada*s (compound words).

2. J — (nivesitaṁ)

   B — n(ivesitaṁ)

   Indraji — namaṁsitaṁ

   The letters *na va sa ta* are sufficiently clear. Since a finite verb is needed to make the meaning of the passage sensible, these letters seem to form *nivesiti*.

   Most probably there is nothing to read between *nivesiti* and *vitadha*. This space was either left out by the scribe due to roughness of the rock or some omission was made by him which necessitated the rubbing of the rock.

3. J — — sabilaṁ(ḍhi)te

   B — (sabipravaji)te

   The characters *sa bi la te* are legible enough. Between *la* and *te* is a character which is more likely *dhi*. They seem to form *sabiladhite* which can mean 'caparisoned horse'.

   Horse was also considered to be an important insignia of royalty. It has, therefore, been bracketted with *makuṭa* (crown).

   This is the last component of the word beginning with *vitadha*. As in the following two words *nikhita* and *hita* govern the remaining components, here *vitadha* governs *makuṭa* and *sabiladhite*.

4. J reads *ca* while B does not.

   It is distinct, as well as necessary for connecting the two principal clauses here.

5. J — ca dānī

   B — cedāni

paṇāḍiṁ Nagaraṁ pavesayati sa . . . .[1] (.) Abhisito ca . . . .[2] rājaseyaṁ[3] saṁdasayaṁto sava-kara-vaṇa[4].

Line 7 anugaha-anekāni sata-sahasāni visajati pora-jānapadaṁ[5] (.) Satame ca vase[6] pasāsato Vajiragharavati-ghusita-gharini s(ā) matuku-pada puṁn(o). . .ta pā. . .[7] (.) Aṭhame ca vase mahatā-senāya

---

1. J — pavesa(ya)ti (.) So......

   B — pavesa(yati) so....... (.)

   Khāravela has given the cost of all of his public works. The mutilated portion ought to contain the cost incurred on the instant work. The sentence would naturally end after mutilation. Since only the initial character is distinct, it is not possible to restore the mutilation and make out the expenses.

2. J — ......bhisito ca

   B — Abhisito (ca)....

   Barua has correctly suggested that the mutilation contained *chaṭhe vase*.

3. J — Rājas(ū)ya(ṁ)

   B & Indraji — rājaseyaṁ

   The following *saṁdasayaṁto* determines the choice.

4. J — — vaṇaṁ

   B — — vaṇa —

5. J — Poraṁ Jānapadaṁ

   B — pora-janapadaṁ

6. J — Satamaṁ ca vasaṁ

   B — Satame ca vase

   All the regnal years in this inscription are given in the form given by Barua. There is no reason for making a departure from the usual practice here.

7. J — pasāsato Vajiraghara-vati-ghusita-gharini sa matuka-padapuṁne.......(Ku)ma. . . . . (.)

   B — (a)sasata-vajiraghara-Khatiya-sata-ghaṭani Samataka-padasaṁna saṁtipada? ? . . . .(.)
   Prinsep & Cunningham — savata-khadapana narapa savitaka-

→

(apati)hata-(bhi)ti-Goradhagiriṁ[1]

Line 8 ghātāpayitā Rājagaha-napa(ṁ) pīḍapayati[2] (.) Etinaṁ[3] ca kaṁmapadāna-panāṁdena[4] saṁbita[5]-senavāhane vipamu(ṁ)citu Madhuraṁ apayāto Yamanā-

---

→ padajhāna-sammatipada(.)

The characters are not so obliterated as to permit such different readings. Only *vati-ghusita* can be alternately read as *Khatiy(ā)-Sat(i)* and by that the meaning retains sense.

In the mutilated portion beyond *puṁno*, two letters are fairly distinct. They are *ta* and *pā*. The context suggests restoration *puṁn(odayā)ta pā(punāti)*.

1. J — sen(ā). . . .Goradhagiriṁ

   B — senāya (apati)hata-(bh)iti-Goradhagiriṁ

2. J — Rājagahaṁ upapīḍāpayati

   B — Rājagaha(ṁ) upapīḍapayati

   Indraji — Rājagaha-napaṁ pīḍāpayatī

   Prinsep — Rājagabhaṁ upapīḍapayati

   Cunningham — Rājagaṁbhu upapīḍapayati

   Konow also read *napa* which is clear enough.

3. J — Etin(ā)
   B — etinaṁ

4. J — sa(ṁ)nādena
   B — panādena

5. J — saṁb(i)ta —
   B — pabaṁta —
   Prinsep — paṁbāta

(nadīṁ)[1]. . .[2] (.) Palavabhāra[3]

Line 9 kaparukha[4] haya-gaja-radha-saha yaṁte sava-gharāvās(ī)-pūji. — Ṭh(ū). —. . ya[5] Sava-gahanaṁ ca

---

1. J — Yavana-rāj(ā) D(i)mi(ta). . .

   B — Yavana-rājā? mi??sa?(ā)mo,

   Since Konow made out *Dimita* the readings of this passage have been generally based on the presumption that it contains a reference to Demetrius, the Greek King. This presumption is, however, not well founded.

   What has hitherto been supposed to read *Yavanarājā*, actually reads *Yamanānadīṁ*. The letters beyond it are indistinct. Barua also thought that *Dimita* could not be definitely made out.

   Yamanā-nadīṁ also fits more appropriately in the context. The verb *apayāto* definitely suggests a geographical point and discounts the possibility of a reference to any person.

2. J — . . . yachati. . . .
   B — dati???. . . .sava(ra)-(rā)jāna ca. . .ga(cha)ti

   The passage is very badly mutilated and it is difficult to make out any reading.

   It should contain words to indicate the direction of the Yamuna river from Kaliṅga or to indicate that the river lay in the Madhya-deśa or something else to qualify it.

   Thereafter there may also be a reference to Khāravela's marching in procession attended by the satellite kings, as is suggested by the reading made out by Barua — *savara-rājāna ca . . . . gachati.* This reading is, however, not free from doubt and can be taken as only a probable.

3. J — palava. . .
   B — palavabhāra

4. J — kapa-rukhe
   B — kapa-rukha —

5. J — sava-gharāvāsa-parivasane agiṇathiyā
   B — sava-gharāvāsa-pa???? ya
   Prinsep — sava-gharavasapa
   Cunn. — sava-gharavasaya-anatikagavaya
   Indraji — sava-gharavasadhaṁ

   The letters after *gharāvāsa* are not quite legible. The syallables *pū ji ṭha* and *ya* can alone be read with some certainty. The space is generally taken to contain 6 to 11 letters. →

kārayituṁ Bamaṇānam jātiṁ parihāraṁ dadāti[1] (,) Arahata ca. . .[2] (.). . . . suvijaya[3]

Line 10 te ubhaya-Prācī-taṭe rāja-nivāsaṁ[4] Mahāvijaya-

→ It is now known that an important Jain Stūpa existed in Mathura in the few centuries preceding the Christian era. A gateway was added to it in the second century BC. By the beginning of the second century AD people started referring to it as '*deva-nirmite*' ('made by gods') due to its long antiquity. It is quite likely that Khāravela worshipped at this Stūpa during his visit to Mathura and also made a note of it in his inscription.

The passage may be restored as follows:

sava-gharāvāsī-pūjita-Ṭhūpa-pūjaya

i.e., 'to worship the *stūpa* worshipped by all the house-holders'.

1. J — Baṁhaṇānaṁ jātiṁ parihāraṁ dadāti
B — bramhaṇānaṁ ja(y)a-parihāraṁ dadāti

The reading *mha* is very doubtful. The character is more clearly *ma*.

2. J — Arahato (va). . .
B — Arahata . . . . .(.)
Ca can be read after *Arahata*. The mutilated portion should supply a verb to govern *Arahata*. The context warrants the following restoration:
Arhata ca pūjati (.)
i.e., 'and worships the Arahat'. For this purpose obviously he should have gone to the *stūpa*.
Here also ends the record of the 8th year.

3. J — (gī)ya(to)

B — . . . . va suvijaya

The event of making successful expedition as far as the Yamuna should have been of great significance for Khāravela and therefore he called it *suvijaya.*

The mutilated portion before *suvijaya* should have contained the words:

Navame ca vase.

Khāravela has recorded the events year-wise and a reference to year is necessary here.

4. J — . . . k.i. mānā(ti)rāja-saṁnivāsaṁ Mahāvijayaṁ pāsādaṁ

B — te ubhaya-Prāci-taṭe(rāja)nivāsaṁ Mahāvijaya-pāsādaṁ

(*Prāci-taṭe* may also be read as *Puti-taṭe* or *Puri taṭe.*)

River Prachi still flows in that region. Therefore the reading *Prācī* can be better relied upon.

pāsādaṁ kārayati aṭhatisāya-sata-sahasehi (.) Dasame ca vase Daṁda-saṁdhī-sā(ma)mayo[1] Bharadavasa-paṭhānaṁ mah(ī)-jayanaṁ . . . . kārāpayati[2] (.) . . . . p(ā)yātānaṁ[3] maniratanāni-saha yāti[4].

Line 11 — (maṁdaṁ) ca Ava-rāja-nivesitaṁ[5] Pithuḍaṁ gadabhanagalena kāsayati[6] (,) janapada-bhāvanaṁ[7]

---

1. J — daṁḍa-saṁdhī-sā(mayo)
   B — dada-ni?dhīta(bhisa)mayo
2. J — mah(ī)-jayanaṁ. . .kārāpayati
   B — ?hi. .?yanaṁ. . . .kārāpayati

   The sentence ends at *kārāpayati.*

   The mutilated portion before *kārāpayati* should have contained some word to mean 'preparations' which were caused to be made by Khāravela.
3. J — . . . . p(ā)yātānaṁ ca

   B— ????? tānaṁ

   The mutilated portion before *pāyātānaṁ* should have contained

   Ekadasame ca vase.

   Ca after *pāyātānaṁ* is obscure as well as redundant.
4. J — upalabhate
   B — saha-yāti
5. J — (maṁdaṁ) ca Ava-rāja-nivesitaṁ
   B — ?? puvarāja-nivesitaṁ

   The initial part of Lines 11-17 has been obliterated. That much space in Lines 1-10 contains 10-12 letters. The best that can now be done to restore the lost text is to make a suggestion in keeping with the context and the size of the space.

   The record of the second year seems to indicate Khāravela's style of describing his expeditions with reference to cardinal points in relation to his dominions. If so, the obliteration here could have contained *dakhina disaṁ,* to mean "in the southern direction".

   The not-so-distinct characters after obliteration strongly suggest *maṁdaṁ,* which also seems to fit in the context.
6. J — Pithuṁḍaṁ gadabha-naṁgalena kāsayati
   B — Pithuḍa gadabha Nagale nekāsayati
7. J — janasa dabhāvanaṁ (janapada-bhāvanaṁ?)
   B — janapada-bhāvanaṁ

ca terasavasa-sata-kataṁ bhiṁdati Tamira-daha-saṁghātaṁ[1] (.) Bārasame ca vase . . . . sa(ha)sehi vitāsayato[2] Utarāpadha-rājāno

Line 12 —[3] Māgadhānaṁ ca vipulaṁ bhayaṁ janeto hathasaṁ Gaṁgāya[4] pāyayati (,) Māgadha(ṁ) ca rājānaṁ Baha(sa)timitaṁ pāde vaṁdāpayati (,) Naṁdarāja-nītaṁ ca Kāliṁga-Jinaṁ saṁnives(e) . . .[5] (,) . . . (gaha)-rata(nā)n(i) paḍīhārehi Aṁga-Magadha-vasuṁ ca neyāti[6] (.)

---

1. J — terasa vasa-satikaṁ ābhi(ṁ)dati T(r)amiradeṣa-saṁghātaṁ

   B — terasa vasa sata-kataṁ bhidati tamiradaha-saṁghātaṁ

   Konow — terasavasa-sata-kata bh(i)dati ———

   Indraji — ——— Tamara-deha saṁghātaṁ

2. J — . . . . hasa ke (saha)-sehi vitāsayati

   B —?s(i)kā(naṁ) sa(ha)-sehi vitāsayaṁto (*or*, vitāsayato)

   The only legible characters are *sahasehi vitāsayato*.

   The mutilated portion before that seems to indicate the agency through which Khāravela struck terror into the hearts of the kings of Uttarāpatha. It could be some feudatory tribe or his own army consisting of thousands of brave warriors. Since he was himself marching at the head of the army and there is also the word *sahasehi*, the latter seems to be more probable. Restoration beyond this suggestion is not feasible.

3. The obliteration could have contained words to mean "while going northwards".

4. J — hathī Sugaṁgīya(ṁ)
   B & Cunn. — hathasaṁ Gaṁgāya
   Prinsep — hathasaṁ Gaṁgasa

5. J — Naṁda rāja-nītaṁ ca Kā(li)ṁga-Jīnaṁ saṁnive(sa). . .

   B — Nadarāja-jita-Kaliṁga-jana-saṁ(n)i(ve)saṁ. . . ?(sasa)ti

   Saṁnivesa should be more correctly read as *saṁnivese*.

   The mutilated portion thereafter should contain the verb *pūjayati*. The composition suggests this restoration.

6. J — . . .(gaha)-rata(nā)na(ṁ) paḍīhārehi Aṁga-Magadha-vasuṁ ca neyāti

→

Line 13 —[1] k(e)tu(ṁ) jaṭhara-lakhila-(go)purāni[2]-siharāni nivesayati sata-visikānaṁ parihārehi[3] (.) Abhutamachariyaṁ ca hathi-nāva-nītaṁ pariharati[4] .... haya-hathi-ratana-māniko[5] Paṁḍa-rājā (cedāni anekāni)[6] muta-maṇi-ratanāni āharāpayati idha sata-sa. . . .[7]

→ B — Kitava-naya-nipu(n)ehi Aga-Magadha-vasuṁ neyāti

Indraji — gaha-ratana-parihārehi ———

The mutilated portion before *gaha* should contain *kosāta*, meaning 'from the Royal Treasury'.

1. The description of the campaign ends in the preceeding line. The mutilation before *ketuṁ* should contain words to mean 'On returning home'. The following activities relate to the capital.
2. J — Katu(ṁ) jaṭhara-l(i)khila barāni

   B — tu(ṁ)ja(ṭha)ra-lakhila-(go)purāni
3. J — sata-visikanaṁ (pa)rihārehi

   B — sata-visikāna(ṁ) parihārena
4. J — hathi-nivā(sa)-parisaraṁ

   (earlier reading — hathi-nāvana)

   B— hathī-nāvataṁ pariharati

   Prinsep — hathi-nāvana

   Cunn. — hathi-navena
5. J — . . . . haya-hathi-ratanā-(mānikaṁ)

   B — tiṁha-haya-hathi-ratana-māniko

   The characters before *haya* are indistinct. The context suggests that the mutilation should supply either a commodity which Khāravela should have seized along with horses, etc., enumerated thereafter or an adverb modifying the verb *pariharati* to mean 'with little difficulty' or 'with great difficulty'.
6. J — c=edāni anekāni

   B — (ābharanaṁ)
7. J — sat(a) . . . .

   B — sata-sa . . . . (restored as *sata-sahasāni*)

   The restoration of Barua is acceptable.

Line 14 — sino[1] vasīkaroti (.) Terasame ca vase supavata-Vijaya-cake-Kumārī-pavate Arahate[2] Pakhiṇa-saṁsitehi Kāya-nisīdīyāy(ā)[3] yāpujavakehi[4] Rāja-bhatin(ā) Cina-vatān(ā) Vasa-sitān(ā)[5] Pūjānurata[6]-uvāsaga-Khāravela-sirinā Jīva-ḍeha-(siritā) parikhātā[7] (.)

---

1. Report of the campaign against the Pāṇḍya King continues. The mutilation should have at least contained *paṁḍa janpadavā*. It can be restored as *Paṁḍa-janapada-vāsino, i.e.*, 'the people of the Pāṇḍya country'.
2. J — arahayate

   B — arahate
3. J — kāya-nisīdīyāya

   B — kayya-nisīdīyāya
4. J — yapa-ñāvakehi

   (earlier reading — yāpujavakehi)

   B — yāpujavakehi, *or*, yāpuravakehi

   Prinsep — yāpuhavakehi

   Cunn. — yāpujakehi
5. J — rāja-bhitini cina-vatāni vās(ā)-s(i)tāni

   B — rāja-bhitini cina-vatāni vāsāsitāni

   The endings of these three words are determined by the following *sirinā*. They are the epithets of Khāravela.
6. J — pūj-anurata —

   B — pūjāya-rata —
7. J — jīva-deha-(siri)kā parikhitā

   B — jīva-deha-??kā . . . . tā (restored as — jīva-deha-sayikā-parikhātā)

Line 15 —[1] sukata[2]-samaṇa-suvihitānaṁ ca sava-disānaṁ[3] ñaninaṁ tapasi-isinaṁ saṁghayanaṁ[4] Arahata-nisīdīyā samīpe pābhāre varākāra-samuthāpitāhi aneka-yojanāhitāhi . . . . silāhi Siṁhapatha-rañī-Siṁdhulāya nisayāni[5] (.)

Line 16 —[6] paṭalake catare[7] ca veḍūriya-gabhe-thabhe[8]

---

1. The missing portion before *sukata* should contain words to mean 'On being invited by King Śrī Khāravela'. It might be: *Nimaṁtitena* (or, *āhutena*) *rājā-Siri-Khāravelena*.
2. J — sukat(ā) —

   B — ? sakata
3. J & B — sata-disānaṁ

   Sircar — sava-disānaṁ
4. J — ñan(i)naṁ tapas(i)-is(i) naṁ saṁghayanaṁ

   B — ñā?naṁ (sama)pasi(naṁ) bhi??-saṁgh(i)yana(ṁ)
5. J — pa si.o . . . . silāhi Siṁhapatha-rañī-Si(ṁ) dhulāya nisayāni

   B — pakva-sisehi (*or*, panata-sisehi) sata-(sahasā)hi silāhi sipaja-thabhā-(ni)vadha-sayanā(sa)nāṁ va

   Prinsep ——— (sapapatha)-dhara-si dhasaya

   The reading of J from *silāhi* to *nisayāni* is highly probable and I accept it as it is also supported by extraneous evidence.

   The mutilated portion between *yojanāhitāhi* and *silāhi* should supply the verb to mean 'assemble'. It may also contain words to show the number of the monks assembled.

   Though it is not free from doubt, *panatisatehi* can be made out after *yojanāhitāhi*. It would mean '3500' and may well indicate the total number of monks who assembled.
6. The mutilation before *paṭalake* should have contained words to mean 'In front of the the Assembly Hall'.
7. J — Paṭalako caturo

   B— paṭalake catare

   Indraji & Cunn. — paṭālake
8. J — veḍūriya-gabhe-thaṁbhe

   B — veḍuriya-gabhe-thabhe

→

patiṭhāpayati (,) pānatariya-saṭha-sata-(va)sehi[1] mukhiya-kala-vochinaṁ[2] ca coyaṭha-Aṁgaṁ saṁtikaṁ[3] turiyaṁ upādayati (.) Khema-rājā sa vadha-rājā[4] sa bhikhu-rājā[5] dhama-rājā pasaṁto sunaṁto anubhavaṁto[6] Kalāṇāni (.)

→ It appears to be the traditional *Mānastambha* (Pride-melting Pillar) which was set up in front of the *Samavasaraṇa* (Preaching Hall) of a Jain *Tīrthaṅkara*. Such pillars are set up in front of Jain temples, particularly in sacred places. Since it was an assembly of monks, it could be appropriately set up in front of the place of assembly. This clue helps restoration before *paṭalake*.

1. J — pānatarīya sata-sahase(hi)

   B — panatariya-(sata-sahasehi)

   The characters other than *va* are fairly readable. There is a little space between *ta* and *se*, and *va* can be restored.

2. J — Muriya-Kāla-vochinaṁ

   B — (ma) khiya-kala-vochine

   Cunn. — . . . . ya-kala

   Indraji — Muriya-kala

3. J — coyaṭh(i) Aṁga-satikaṁ

   B — coyaṭha-aṁge satikaṁ

   Prinsep — coyaṭha agi satika

   Cunn. — coyaṭha age satika

   Indraji — coyaṭha age satiku

4. J — Vadha-rājā

   B — vadha-rājā

5. J — Bhikhu-rājā

   B — bhikhu-rājā sa (,)

6. J — pasaṁt(o) sunat(o) anubhavat(o)

   B — pasaṁto sunato anubhavaṁto

   Ṁ in *sunaṁto* is determined by the other two words immediately preceding and following it.

Line 17 —[1] Guṇa-visesa-kusalo Sava-pāsaṁḍa-pūjako Sava-devāyatana-saṁkhārakārako[2] Apatihata-caka-vāhana-balo[3] Caka-dharo Guta-cako[4] Pavata-cako Rājasi-vaṁsa-kula-viniśito[5] Mahāvijayo Rājā-Khāravela-Siri (.)

---

1. The style of the epigraph strongly suggests that this mutilation should have contained the date of this record. It is the beginning of the concluding line and what follows the mutilation is the name of the king with his many epithets, apparently with no other purpose except as if he had put his signatures at the end of the notification. Khāravela is very particular in giving dates. He has noted the events of his reign regnal-year-wise. He has also given the dates of some of the major historical events like the founding of the Tamila Confederacy, the opening of the Tanasuliyavāṭā Canal and the decline of the Principal Scripture. He could certainly not leave his record incomplete by omitting the date of its recording. This date should have been in the same era in which he has given the dates of other major historical events. But unfortunately we cannot make out the recorded date due to the vagaries of Nature.

   The space could have contained 12-13 syllables which could make 'Pānatariya-panatisata-vasa', to mean 'the year 355' in M.E. which, as we shall see below, can be deduced as the date of this epigraph.

2. J — sava-de(v-āya)tana-saṁkhārakārako

   B — sava-devāyatana sa(ṁ)kārakārako

3. J — (a)patihata-caki-vāhini-balo

   B — apatihata-caka-vāhana-balo

4. J — Caka-dhura-guta-cako

   B — Caka-dharo guta-cako

5. J — rājasi-Vasū-kula-viniśrito

   B — rājisi-vaṁsa-kula-vini(śr)ito, *or*, vini(g)ito

   In *viniśito* the character is more clearly *śi* than anything else. It is neither *śri* nor *gi*.

Translation

On the basis of the above reading and proposed restorations it should be rendered into English as follows.* The restorations have been shown within [ ] and the explanatories within ( ).

"Obeisance to the *Arahaṁtas*!
Obeisance to all the *Siddhas*!!

By the Hon'ble King, Mahāmeghavāhana, His Majesty Khāravela, the Lord of Kaliṅga, the Increaser of Ceti Royal House, (the Owner of) glorifying auspicious marks, (and) the Possessor of virtues (the fame of which has) reached the farthest limits of the four quarters, were played for fifteen years, with a

---

* **Jayaswal and Banerji (*E.I.*, XX, pp. 86-89) and Barua (*I.H.Q.*, XIV, 3, pp. 470—82) give different renderings. Below, J stands for Jayaswal & Banerji, and B for Barua.**

J — L1 Salutation to the Arhats (*Arihats* lit. 'Conquerors of Enemies', *i.e.,* Jinas). Salutation to all the Siddhas. By illustrious Khāravela, the Aira (Aiḷa), the Great King, the descendant of Mahāmeghavāhana, the increaser (of the glory) of the Ceti (Cēdi) dynasty, (endowed) with excellent and auspicious marks and features, possessed of virtues which have reached (the ends of) four quarters, overlord of Kaliṅga,

L 2 for fifteen years, with a body ruddy and handsome were played youthsome sports; after that (by him who) had mastered (royal) correspondence, currency, finance, civil and religious laws (and) who had become well-versed in all (branches) of learning, for nine years (the office of) Yuvarāja (heir-apparent) was administered. Having completed the twenty-fourth

---

B — "Obeisance to Arhats, the Exalted Ones, obeisance to all Siddhas, the Perfect Saints.

By His Graceful Majesty Khāravela, the great Aira king, the Sovereign lord of Kaliṅga, the scion of the Mahāmegha family, the increaser of the

body handsome and tawny in colour, sports (worthy of) Prince.

Thereafter by the Adept in Correspondence, Currency, Accountancy, State Regulations and Laws, (and) the Clear-headed in all Sciences, (the kingdom) was administered for nine years as Crown Prince.

Then on completing the twenty-fourth year, to make the remainder of his youth prosperous by conquests, being the third in descent in the Royal House of Kaliṅga, (he) gets anointed as Great King.

And, having been anointed, in the first year (of his reign), (he) causes in the capital of Kaliṅga, (verily) the Abode of the Brave, the gates, ramparts and buildings, which had been

---

J — year, at that time, (he) who had been prosperous (*vardhamāna*) since his infancy (?) and who (was destined) to have wide conquests as those of Vena,

L 3 then in the state of manhood, obtains the imperial (māhārājya) coronation in the third dynasty of Kaliṅga.

B — Ceti Royal House, who is possessed of the noble and auspicious marks, who is gifted with the attributes (of one capable) of subduing the earth extending as far as the four seas, were played for fifteen years the sports befitting the young age of the prince with a handsome body of 'fair brown complexion'. Thereafter, for nine years, just the office of a Crown Prince was administered by (His Royal Highness) who was well-versed in (matters relating to) writing, coinage, accounting, procedure, and approved principle of action, whose self was purified by proficiency in all (Indian) 'polite learning'. Having then completed twenty-four years, he who, as he waxed great, passed the rest of his manhood in making notable conquests, gained the high state implied by the coronation of a great king in the third royal dynasty of Kaliṅga, in regular linear succession.

And as soon as he was anointed, in the very first year, (His Majesty) caused the Kaliṅga-city Khibīra in which the gates, walls and residential houses were damaged by stormy wind, to be repaired, and caused the

damaged by storm, to be repaired, and the embankments of the cool reservoir to be strengthened, and all the parks to be renovated, by (spending) thirty-five hundred thousands; and (he) makes (his) subjects happy.

And in the second year (of his reign), paying no heed to (King) Śātakarṇi (he) sends in the western direction a multitudinous army (consisting of) cavalry, elephants, infantry and chariots, and with his army having reached the (river) Kr̥ṣṇaveṇā, strikes terror into the capital of the Asikas.

Again, in the third year (of his reign), the Master of the Science of Music makes (the citizens of) the capital enjoy themselves by causing the performance of folk dances, (classical) dances, songs and instrumental music, and the celebration of festivals and fairs.

Likewise, in the fourth year (of his reign), (he) dwells in the Dwellings of the Vidyādharas (which) no former king of Kaliṅga had ever scathed, and makes all the Raṭhikas and Bhojakas (whose) crown and caparisoned horse have been dashed to

---

J — As soon as he is anointed, in the first (regnal) year (he) causes repairs of the gates, the walls and the buildings (of the city), (which had been) damaged by storm; in the city of Kaliṅga (he) causes the erection of the embankments of the lake (called after) Khibīra R̥ṣi, (and) of (other) tanks and cisterns, (also) the restoration of all the gardens (he) causes to be

L 4 done at (the cost of) thirty-five hundred thousands, and, (he) gratifies the People. And in the second year (he), disregarding Sātakaṁni, despatches to the western regions an army strong in cavalry, elephants, infantry (*nara*) and chariots (*ratha*) and by that army having reached the Kañha-beṁṇā, (he) throws the city of the Musikas into consternation. Again in the third year,

---

B — embankments of the cool tanks to be made and (also) caused the work of restoration of all the gardens to be done at the cost of thirty-five hundred thousand (pieces of the standard coin), and (thereby) pleased the subjects.

pieces, umbrella and golden pitcher have been removed and jewels and fortune have been seized, to bow down at (his) feet.

And, in the fifth bountiful year (of his reign), (he) causes the Tanasuliyavāṭā Canal (which was) opened out by the Nanda king in the year 103, to be brought into the capital [by spending . . . thousands].

And, having been anointed [for six years], to display (his) royal opulence (he) bestows all taxes, grants and many (other) favours (worth) hundreds and thousands upon the townsmen and villagers.

J — L 5 (he) versed in the science of the Gandharvas (*i.e.*, music), entertains the capital with the exhibition of *dapa*, dancing, singing and instrumental music and by causing to be held festivities and assemblies (*samājas*); similarly in the fourth year, 'the Abode of Vidyādharas' built by the former Kaliṅga king(s), which had not been damaged before . . . . with their coronets rendered meaningless, with their helmets(?) (*bilma*) cut in twain (?), and with their umbrellas and

L 6 *bhiṅgāras* cast away, deprived of their jewels (*i.e.*, *ratana*, Skt. *ratna*, precious objects) all the Raṭhikas and Bhojakas (he) causes to bow down at his feet. Now in the fifth year he brings into the capital from the road of Tanasuliya the canal excavated in the year one-hundred-and-three of

---

B — And in the second year, not (at all) bringing Śātakarṇi into (his) thought, (His Majesty) caused a multitudinous army (consisting of) horses, elephants, foot-men and chariots to march in a western direction, and with the aid of the army that reached (the bank of) the Kr̥ṣṇaveṇā (river), struck terror into the city of Asika (Musika?).

Again, in the third year, (His Majesty) who was a master of the science of music — the Gandharva lore, caused the capital to be entertained by the display of combats, dancing, singing,and instrumental music, and (no less) by the arrangements made for festivities and convivial gatherings.

Likewise, in the fourth year, (His Majesty caused to be done his duty to) the home of the Vidyādharas, founded by the former kings of Kaliṅga, which was not invaded before, compelled all the Raṭhikas and Bhojakas,

And, while reigning in the seventh year, she, (that is, his) wife named Vajiragharavati, [obtains] the dignity of mother [due to] accumulated merit.

And, in the eighth year (of his reign), having stormed the invulnerable Gorathagiri (fortress) with a big army (he) oppresses the king of Rājagṛha. And sounding aloud this act of prowess (he), along with (his) army and entourage, marches to the river Yamuna [lying in the...] having liberated (the city of) Mathura. [And (he) moves with satellite kings. (?)] (Here), with a Wish-fulfilling Tree burdened with foliage, and along with (his) cavalry, elephants and chariots, (he) goes [to worship the Stūpa] reverenced by all householders and, having performed the

---

J — King Nanda. . . . Having been (re-)anointed (he while) celebrating the Rājasūya, remits all tithes and cesses,

L 7 bestows many privileges (amounting to) hundreds of thousands on the City-Corporation and the Realm-Corporation. In the seventh year of his reign, his famous wife of Vajiraghara obtained the dignity of auspicious motherhood. . . . Then in the eighth year (he) with a large army having sacked Goradhagiri,

L 8 causes pressure on Rājagaha (Rājagṛha). On account of the loud report of this act of valour, the Yavana (Greek) King Dimi(ta) retreated to Mathura having extricated his demoralised army and transport . . . . (He) gives . . . . with foliage,

L 9 Kalpa (Wish-fulfilling) trees, elephants, chariots with their drivers, houses, residences and rest-houses. And to make all these acceptable

---

B — who were deprived of their wealth and jewels, whose royal insignia consisting of umbrellas and vases had been cast away, who were abandoned by good Brahmins(?), and whose crowns were rendered meaningless, to bow down at (his) feet.

And then in the fifth year, (His Majesty) caused the canal opened out by King Nanda three hundred (or 103) years back to be brought into the capital from the Tanasuliya road. . . .

And in the sixth year, (His Majesty) while displaying his royal prosperity, bestowed (unprecedented) favours on the inhabitants of towns and

Sarva-grahaṇa (ceremony), gives the community of Brahmins gifts and [worships] the *Arahaṁta*.

After the well (accomplished campaign of) conquest, [in the ninth year (of his reign)], (he) builds the royal abode named Mahāvijayaprāsāda on both the banks of the (river) Prachi by (spending) thirty-eight hundred thousands.

And, in the tenth year (of his reign), the Dispenser of War and Peace causes to be made [preparations] (for) marching forth in Bhāratavarṣa to conquer the (whole) land.

J — (he) gives at a fire Sacrifice (?) exemption (from taxes) to the caste of Brāhmaṇas. Of Arhat. . . .

L 10 . . . .(He) causes to be built . . . a royal residence (called) the Palace of Great Victory (*Mahāvijaya*) at the cost of thirty-eight hundred thousands. And in the tenth year (he), following (the three-fold policy) of chastisement, alliance and conciliation sends out an expedition against Bharatavasa (and) brings about the conquest of the land (or, country) . . . and obtains jewels and precious things of the (kings) attacked.

B — districts by remitting all taxes and duties amounting to many hundred thousands (pieces of the standard coin).

And in the seventh year, (His Majesty caused) compact groups of hundreds of horses, (portable) 'diamond chambers' and warriors (to proceed to) the tranquil spot adjoining the foot of the Samataka (hill) (?). . . .

And in the eight year, having stormed with a mighty army (the fortress of) Gorathagiri of invulnerable wall, (His Majesty) brought a pressure to bear upon Rājagṛha, and the Yavana King? mi???? retreated to Mathura in order to release the troops and vehicles restlessly moving on account of the uproar of reprisal on his (Majesty's) part . . . . returned (to Kaliṅga), marched back with Kalpavṛksha, the Wishing Tree, burdened with foliage, and (the troops) of horses, elephants and chariots, (did something for) all householders, and to captivate all (he) offered the gift of victory to the Brahmins, (offered something to) the Ārhata (recluses). . . .

[And, in the eleventh year (of his reign)], (carrying) with (him) gems and jewels (he) moves [in the southern direction] in a slow procession and causes Pithuṇḍa, the abode of Ava kings, to be ploughed by ploughs drawn by asses, and for the well-being of (his) realm, breaks the confederacy of Tamila countries (which had been) formed in the year 113.

And, in the twelfth year (of his reign), [marching at the head of] thousands [of brave warriors], (he) strikes terror into (the hearts of) the kings of Uttarāpatha [while going northward], and engendering great fear into (the hearts of) the people of Magadha, causes (his) elephants and horses to drink (water) in the (river) Ganga, and makes the king of Magadha, (named) Bahasatimita, to bow down at (his) feet, and [worships] in the temple (enshrining the image) of Jina from Kaliṅga (which had been) taken away (from there) by the Nanda king, and having seized the family-jewels [from the treasury], carries away the riches of Aṅga and Magadha.

J — L 11. . . . . And the market-town(?) Pithuṁḍa founded by the Ava King he ploughs down with a plough of asses; and (he) thoroughly breaks up the confederacy of the T(r)amira (Dramira) countries of one hundred and thirteen years, which has been a source of danger to (his) Country (Janapada). And in the twelfth year he terrifies the kings of the Uttarāpatha with . . . . thousands of

L 12 . . . . And causing panic amongst the people of Magadha (he) drives (his) elephants into the Sugaṁgīya (Palace) and (he) makes the king of Magadha, Bahasatimita, bow at his feet. And (he) sets up (the image) 'the Jina of Kaliṅga' which had been taken away by King Nanda . . . and causes to be brought home the riches of Aṅga and Magadha along with the keepers of the family jewels of . . . .

B — And in the ninth year, (His Majesty) caused the royal residence Mahāvijaya-prāsāda, the "Great Victory Palace", to be built on both the banks of Prācī at the cost of thirty-eight hundred thousand (pieces of the standard coin).

And in the tenth year, well-read and experienced in the principles of policy, (His Majesty) proceeded on a campaign for the conquest of countries in Bhāratavarṣa . . . .(?)

[On returning home], (he) causes banners to be fixed on all the firm pinnacles of the gates (of the capital) by spending two thousand. And (it is) portentous marvel (that) leading (a force of) elephants and boats (he) seizes [with little difficulty] horses, elephants, jewels and rubies from the king of the Pāṇḍyas and at this moment fetches many pearls, gems and jewels (worth) hundreds and [thousands], and subjugates [the people of the Pāṇḍya kingdom].

And, in the thirteenth year (of his reign), by the Royal Worshipper (who has) performed the vows (and is) resplendent with (supernatural) powers, the Lay Devotee (who is) addicted to worship, His Majesty Khāravela (whose) soul is dependent on body, is caused to be excavated for purposes of worship the Relic Memorial (in honour of) the *Arahaṁta*s (who have) cast off transmigration, on Mount Kumārī, the auspicious mountain in Vijaya circle.

[On being invited by the King, His majesty Khāravela], the Reverend Śramaṇas (who are) self-possessed and the *Jñānī*s, *Tapasvī-Ṛṣi*s and leaders of *Saṁgha*s from all directions, (coming from) many *yojana*s, [numbering thirty-five hundred, assemble]

J — L 13 . . . . .(He) builds excellent towers with carved interiors and creates a settlement of a hundred masons, giving them exemption from land revenue. And wonderful and marvellous enclosure of stockade for driving in the elephants (he) . . . and horses, elephants, jewels and rubies as well as numerous pearls in hundreds (he) causes to be brought here from the Pāṇḍya King.

L 14 . . . . (he) subjugates. In the thirteenth year, on the Kumārī Hill where the wheel of Conquest had been well-revolved (*i.e.*, the religion of Jina had

---

B — And in the eleventh year, (His Majesty). . . .went in procession with jewels and gems. . . . caused the grassy overgrowth of Pṛthudaka, founded by a former king, to be let out into the Lāṅgala (river) and destroyed the accumulation of dark swamps that grew up in thirteen-and-hundred years (and) became a cause of anxiety to the country.

And in the twelfth year, ... with the aid of thousands of the Śivis(?), (His Majesty) produced consternation among the rulers of Uttarāpatha,

in the well-laid out quadrangle near the shrine of the *Arahaṁta* on the top of the hill, on the stone (platform adjacent to) the shrine (dedicated by) Queen Sindhulā (hailing from) Siṁhapatha.

[In front of the Assembly Hall] (he) causes to be set up a pale red and quadrilateral pillar inlaid with beryl, and causes to be read expeditiously the peace-giving Principal Scripture,

---

J — been preached), (he) offers respectfully royal maintenances, China clothes (silks) and white clothes to (the monks) who (by their austerities) have extinguished the round of lives, the preachers on the religious life and conduct at the Relic Memorial. By Khāravela, the illustrious, as a layman devoted to worship, is realised (the nature of) *jīva* and *deha.*

L 15 . . . bringing about a Council of the wise ascetics and sages, from hundred (*i.e.*, all) quarters, the monks (Samaṇas) of good deeds and who have fully followed (the injunctions) . . . . near the Relic Depository of the

---

B — while generating an immense fear among the people of Magadha, caused the elephants and horses to drink in the Ganges, and compelled Bṛhaspatimitra, the king of the Magadha people, to bow down at his feet, (did something in connection with) the settlements of the Kaliṅga people subjugated by King Nanda . . . . carried the wealth of Aṅga and Magadha with the aid of persons skilled in clever tactics,. . . . caused to be erected towering temples and gates with figures of the goddess of luck in their niches, procured at the cost of a hundred *viśas* (of gold) the rare and wonderful trappings of elephants, the King of Pāṇḍya, rich in mettled horses, elephants and jewels and gems supplied here hundreds and thousands of apparel(?), pearls, gems and jewels, ... subdued (some people).

And in the thirteenth year, on the Kumārī hill in the well-founded realm of Victory, were excavated the *jīvadehaśrayikās* by His Graceful Majesty Khāravela, devoted to the worship of those who depended on royal patronage, those who had fulfilled their (religious) vows, (and) those who sought shelter during the rains for use as comfortable resting places by the Ārhata (recluses), the cause of whose future gliding in the course of transmigration had been greatly extenuated (and) who were (there) for fulfilling the Yāpa (Rainy Season Vow).

(that is,) the Twelve *Aṅgas*, (which has been) gradually declining (in volume) since the year 165. He (is a) peaceful king, he (is a) wise king, (a) mendicant king (and a) righteous king (who) questions about, listens to (and) meditates upon the well-meaning scriptures.

J — Arhat, on the top of the hill, ... with stones ... brought from many miles (*yojanas*) quarried from excellent mines (he builds) shelters for the Siṁhapatha Queeen Sindhulā. ...

L 16 .... Paṭalaka(?) .... (he) sets up four columns inlaid with beryl ... at the cost of seventy-five hundred thousands; (he) causes to be compiled expeditiously the (text) of the seven-fold Aṁgas of the sixty-four (letters). He is the King of Peace, the King of Prosperity, the King of Monks (*bhikṣus*), the King of Religion (*Dharma*), who has been seeing, hearing, and realising blessings (*Kalyāṇas*) —

B — For the honoured recluses of well-established reputation and the Jñātṛkas (?) viewing all things alike (and) the monks(?) belonging to (different) orders (and) coming from a hundred directions, with hundreds and thousands of stones quarried out of excellent quarries (and) collected from (an area extending over) many *yojanas* by expert heads, (His Majesty caused) indeed (to be made) sleeping-and-sitting accommodations fitted with artistic pillars(?) on a slope near the Ārhata resting place, and caused the columns to be set up in a beryl-set hall with an ornamental courtyard at the cost of seventy-five hundred thousand (pieces of the standard coin), and in sixty-four panels, intersected with sculptures, caused to be produced (the scenes of) peaceful music.

The king of severity was he, the king of prosperity, the king of renunciation, the righteous king, (capable) of perceiving, hearing and

[The year. . .] The Expert in extraordinary excellences, the Worshipper of all religions, the Embellisher of all temples, the (Possesser of the) might of irresistible army and entourage, the Bearer of the Wheel (of conquest), the Protector of the realm, (the One) whose wheel rolls on unimpeded, the Support of princely houses and families, the Great Conqueror, His Majesty Khāravela the King."

J — L.17 . . . . accomplished in extra-ordinary virtues, respector of every sect, the repairer of all temples, one whose chariot and army are irresistible, one whose empire is protected by the chief of the empire (himself), descended from the family of the Royal Sage Vasū, the Great Conqueror, the King, the illustrious Khāravela."

B — experiencing things that are conducive to welfare was His Graceful Majesty Khāravela, the mighty conqueror, the upholder of the realm of royal command, the protector of the realm of royal command, the repairer of all abodes of the gods, the worshipper of all sects, accomplished by virtue of the possession of certain special qualities."

2

The Date of the Inscription and its Author

AN analysis of the data presented in this epigraph gives us much valuable information not only about the personality and achievements of Khāravela, but also about the political and social conditions of the times in which he lived. The most baffling problem about him is, however, his date.

This is the earliest known inscription which mentions dates of past historical events. The Tanasuliyavāṭā canal is stated to have been opened by the Nanda King in *ti-vasa-sata* or the year 103, the Tamila Confederacy is stated to have been formed in *terasa-vasa-sata* or the year 113, and the Principal Scripture of the Jains is stated to be declining in volume since *pānatariya-saṭha-sata-vasa* or the year 165. The question arises — in what era are these dates mentioned?

The circumstance that the inscription was incised on the occasion of a religious ceremony, lends the clue that the era of reckoning may be one connected with the religion to which the ceremony related. It leads us to assume that these dates are in the Mahāvīra Era which has been as much popular among the Jains as the *Anno Domini* among the Christians or the *Anno Hegira* among the Muslims. The M.E. is said to have started from October 15, 527 BC, the date of *nirvāṇa* or demise, the last memorable event in the life of Mahāvīra, the last of the twenty-four *Tīrthaṅkaras* reverenced by the Jains.[1]

---

1. For a discussion of the date of Mahāvīra's *nirvāṇa*, see Jain, Dr. J.P., →

Taken in M.E. the above three events would fall in 424 BC, 414 BC, and 362 BC, respectively.

The extant literary traditions of both the Digambaras and the Śvetāmbaras, the principal sects among the Jains, seem to confirm that the date for gradual decline of the canonical knowledge may be M.E. 165. According to the Digambaras as well as the Śvetāmbaras eight pontiffs after Mahāvīra possessed full canonical knowledge and the last of them was Bhadrabāhu I. The Digambaras assign a period of 162 years to these eight pontiffs, while the Śvetāmbaras assign 178 years.[1] It is possible that the period was actually 165 years since the tradition recorded in this inscription is closer to the event than any of the available literary traditions.

As for placing the event of the opening of the Tanasuliyavāṭā canal in M.E. 103 or 424 BC, it is necessary to consider the chronology of Nanda. Nanda is twice mentioned in this inscription: he opened the canal in the year 103 and he took away the image of Jina from Kaliṅga to Magadha. It means that this Nanda was the King of Magadha. The Jain tradition unanimously places the Nandas 60 years after Mahāvīra and assigns them a rule of 155 or 150 years. This is with reference to Ujjayinī[2] and indicates that the Nanda kings of Magadha had annexed Ujjayinī in 467 BC. The expression *Naṁda-rāja* used in the inscription also seems to indicate that it does not refer to a particular King Nanda; it more correctly refers to a Nanda king, *i.e.*, a king of the Nanda dynasty. The Nandas continued to rule in Ujjayinī till 312 or 317 BC, when the Mauryas dislodged them. Candragupta Maurya's coup in Magadha is dated in *circa* 324 BC. He may have taken some time to

→ *The Jaina Sources of the History of Ancient India*, pp. 32-54; also Appendix III *infra*.

A *Tīrthaṅkara* is a religious pioneer and deified saint.

1. J.P. Jain, *op. cit.*, pp. 262-65 (Pontifical Genealogy of Mahāvīra's Successors).
2. *Ibid.*, pp. 255-61, (Dynastic Chronology from Mahāvīra's *nirvāṇa* to M.E. 1000).

consolidate his position in Magadha and may have been able to extend his sway over Ujjayinī a few years later. The Maurya chronology does not cause any hindrance in assuming that the Nandas ruled over Ujjayinī for 155 or 150 years after 60 years from the demise of Mahāvīra.

As for reconciling this period with the history of Magadha, the seat of the Nanda imperial authority, it is significant that the Brahmanical Purāṇas assign a total of 143 years to Mahānandin, and Mahāpadma and his eight sons. On the basis of Candragupta Maurya's accession in 324 BC, the Nanda dynasty's rule in Magadha ended in that year and the accession of Mahānandin took place in 467 BC. Since the Jain and Brahmanical traditions converge on this point, Mahānandin may be taken to be the founder of the Nanda dynasty.[1]

The Buddhist tradition is firm on the point that the Buddha's death took place in the eighth year of Ajātaśatru's reign. It also assigns a total of 80 years to Ajātaśatru and his successors, *i.e.*, a total of 72 years after the Buddha. The Brahmanical tradition assigns a total of 83 years to them. The traditional date of the Buddha's demise is 544 BC.[2] On that basis Ajātaśatru's line

---

1. The total period of 143 years for the Nanda rule in Magadha seems to be correctly represented by Mahānandin (43 years), Mahāpadma (88 years) and Mahāpadma's 8 sons (12 years). Nandivardhana (40 years) is said to have preceded Mahānandin and he is also said to have founded the Nanda line. It, however, appears that Nandivardhana and Mahānandin are identical, the latter ('the Great Nanda') being a title of the former. Al-Beruni mentions an Indian era with the initial year 458 BC, which goes back to the time of the first Nanda king (see Sachau, E.C., *Al-Beruni's India*, II, pp. 5-7). This also seems to suggest that the Nanda take-over in Magadha might be in 467 BC. The era might have been founded a decade later to commemorate the assumption of imperial status.

2. This is according to the oldest tradition among the Buddhists. Geiger places the event in 483 BC on the basis of a late Cantonese tradition. It is worth noticing that while the historians have generally placed implicit reliance on the Sri Lankanese Buddhist traditions for the

→

should come to an end in 472 or 469 BC. It also brings us nearer 467 BC for the beginning of the Nanda rule.

It appears that there was an interregnum of 3 to 5 years before Mahānandin could firmly establish himself in Magadha and soon after he launched Magadha on an ambitious career of conquest. In 424 BC Mahāpadma succeeded him and he appears to have led the victorious arms of Magadha into Kaliṅga and further south. The inauguration of one's reign with a campaign of conquest, has been a popular practice with ambitious monarchs throughout the world. It is also reflected in Khāravela's desire at the time of his coronation 'to make the remainder of his youth prosperous by making conquests'.

In the very first year of his reign, in 424 BC, Mahāpadma conquered Kaliṅga, opened the Tanasuliyavāṭā canal there, and took away the image of Jina from Kaliṅga to Magadha. He may have marched further south and subjugated the Tamila kingdoms of the far south. This must have been quite unexpected for them and so the idea of forming a confederacy should have dawned upon them. According to the instant inscription this confederacy was formed in 414 BC, ten years after Mahāpadma Nanda's campaign in Kaliṅga.

This confederacy arrested the southward expansion of the Magadha empire under the Nandas and after them, under the Mauryas. On the basis of the evidence afforded by the

→ chronological build-up of Magadha from Bimbisāra to Aśoka, they have rejected the same for the date of the Buddha himself. This has been done on the basis of Sandrokottos-Candragupta Maurya synchronism and by computing the dates from Candragupta's accession to and fro. Perhaps it would be better to reconcile the points of general agreement in the different sets of traditions (Jain, Buddhist and Brahmanical) on the basis of certain firm points in those traditions. When worked on that method, a reasonable chronology can be drawn out for ancient India. I am inclined to support the traditional dates of the Buddha and Mahāvīra as preserved in the respective Buddhist and Jain traditions since they would hardly make a mistake on that point. Also see Appendix III *infra*.

inscriptions of Aśoka Maurya it can be assumed that the Magadha empire had extended as far south as the Godavari and the Krishna rivers. This region appears to have been brought under the Magadha empire by the Nandas, most probably Mahāpadma whose depredations led the Tamilas to form a confederacy. Reference to the Nandas in the early *Saṅgam* literature, the oldest Tamil literature, lends support to this assumption.[1]

In Rock Edicts II and XIII Aśoka lists the Colas, the Pāṇḍyas, the Satiyaputras, the Keralaputras and the Tāmraparṇīyas (Sri Lankanese) as living to the south of his empire. They seem to represent the members of the Tamila Confederacy. The Confederacy not only held its own against the Magadha imperialism under the Nandas and Mauryas, but in course of time itself became a danger to its neighbours. This is suggested by Khāravela's motive in breaking it in his eleventh regnal year. He did it 'for the well-being of his realm'. And he could think of marching against the Pāṇḍya king in the twelfth year only after he had broken the Confederacy in the previous year, probably through diplomatic means.

The above discussion strongly suggests that the dates mentioned in the instant inscription are in M.E.

Unfortunately the date of the epigraph itself is missing. It has already been suggested in fn. 1 on p. 22 *ante* that the mutilation at the beginning of L 17 should have, in all probability, contained it. Under the existing circumstances, however, we have to ascertain it on the basis of the contemporary data available in the inscription.

Names of two contemporaries are mentioned: Sātakaṁniṁ in the western direction, and Bahasatimitaṁ, the king of Magadha; the former with reference to an event in the second year of his reign, and the latter, to that in the twelfth year. Added to this is the fact that Khāravela was the third ruler of his dynasty, the *Cedi-rāja-vaṁsa*.

1. Sastri, K.A.N., *A History of South India*, (2nd edn., 1958), pp. 85-86.

It is generally accepted now that the Maurya Empire disintegrated soon after the death of Aśoka in *c.* 235-234 BC. His grandsons Daśaratha, Samprati and Vigatāśoka seem to have divided the empire among themselves with their centres respectively in Magadha, Ujjayinī and Gandhāra. Jalauka, a son of Aśoka, also seems to have become independent in Kashmir. Taking advantage of the internecine feuds among the successors of Aśoka, some of his servants also appear to have carved out independent principalities. The examples seem to be furnished by the founder of the Sātavāhana line in the Nasik region and the founder of the Cedi line in the Kaliṅga region.

According to Prof. K.A.N. Sastri, 'the exact date of the foundation of Sātavāhana power cannot be determined, but the puranic lists suggest that the first king, Simuka, probably began to reign about 230 BC'.[1] Dr. K. Gopalachari more surely places the event soon after Aśoka's death in *c.* 235 BC.[2]

The Sātvāhanas have been referred to as 'Āndhrabhṛtya' which further suggests that the founder of the line was a servant of the Maurya emperors, perhaps of the rank of a Mahāmātra (member of the Imperial Service) and holding a Commissioner's or Governor's charge in the region where he proclaimed his independence, and that he originally belonged to the Andhra region.[3] In no other way the Sātavāhanas appear to be connected with Andhra; all their possessions were confined to the western coast and only a very late epigraph of the 24th or 26th ruler is

---

1. *Op. cit.*, p. 89.
2. *A Comprehensive History of India*, II, pp. 293-328.

   Gurty Venkat Rao's view placing Simuka in 271 BC is highly improbable. No such thing could be thought of in the hey-day of Maurya imperial power under Aśoka. The political geography available in Aśoka's epigraphs also discounts such a hypothesis. (Rao in *The Early History of the Deccan*, pt. I-VI, pp. 90ff.).
3. Sudhakar Chattopadhyaya has discussed the controversy as regards the home of the Sātavāhanas in the *Journal of Indian History*, XLI, 3, (December 1963), pp. 749-55. He also holds that the Sātavāhanas were migrants to the Maharashtra region.

the earliest Sātavāhana record so far known from the Krishna district in Andhra Pradesh on the eastern coast.

The founder of the Sātavāhana line was Simuka who is assigned a reign of 23 years. He was succeeded by his younger brother Kṛṣṇa (Kanha) who reigned for 18 years. Then came Śrī Śātakarṇi whose exploits are recorded in the Nanaghat inscriptions of his queen Nāgānikā. He reigned for ten years (*c*. 194-184 BC). He is said to have been a very powerful king who performed many sacrifices including the *Rājasūya* and the *Aśvamedha* which proclaim political supremacy and ascendancy.

Two facts strongly suggest that this Śātakarṇi should be the Sātakaṁniṁ of the instant epigraph. The passage *acitayitā-Sātakaṁniṁ* indicates that Śātakarṇi was a powerful ruler with considerable influence to the west of Kaliṅga and it was really a matter of great courage not to pay any heed to him and send troops in the western direction. On the basis of the available evidence Śrī Śātakarṇi appears to have possessed such influence and power, but his namesake, the sixth ruler of the line who came 36 years after him, is not credited with any military or political exploits. The tenor of the inscription suggests that Khāravela was a man of action himself and would not have referred to anybody in such a rather deferential tone unless he was convinced of his superiority as a man of action. The event relates to the second year of Khāravela's reign. A year later he himself marches into the Vindhyas and subdues the Raṭhikas and Bhojakas, the feudatory chiefs most probably owing allegiance to the Sātavāhanas and at least under their influence. This seems to indicate that the power of the Sātavāhanas had rather suddenly declined by that time. Khāravela did not come into direct conflict with the Sātavāhanas most probably because they were remote from his dominions. This discussion leads us to the conclusion that the 2nd regnal year of Khāravela should coincide with the 10th or 9th year of Śātakarṇi's reign, *i.e.*, 184 or 185 BC.

The other fact supporting this synchronism is that a total

of 50 years had elapsed by then since the founding of the Sātavāhana and Cedi lines. The latter was founded by the grandfather of Khāravela and that much period is not improbable for the two reigns, of his grandfather and father. If this Śātakarṇi is taken to be the sixth (instead of the third) ruler of the Sātavāhana line, the beginning of whose reign is placed 18 or 36 years later, the intervening period between Khāravela's accession and the founding of the line by his grandfather would be at least 68 years or 86 years even if the 2nd year of his reign is supposed to be the very first year of that Śātakarṇi's reign. The fact that Khāravela himself was coronated at the age of 24, however, lends support to the assumption that the total period of the reigns of his grandfather and father could not have been greater than 50 years.

We may conclude that the coronation of Khāravela took place 50 years after the disintegration of the Maurya Empire at the death of Aśoka, that the first Śātakarṇi, the third ruler of the Sātavāhana dynasty, was his contemporary, and that this Śātakarṇi's reign came to an end before Khāravela launched his successful campaign in the Vindhyas in his 4th regnal year. It would mean that Khāravela's reign began in *c.* 185 BC and the date of the instant inscription, which was recorded in the 13th regnal year of Khāravela, should be *c.* 172 BC or ME 355.[1] Since there is no further record of Khāravela it is possible that his reign might have come to an end in that year. The palaeographic similarities of the instant inscription with the Nanaghat inscriptions of Śrī Śātakarṇi's queen Nāgānikā, may be cited as a further supporting evidence for the above view.

But the identification of Bahasatimitaṁ presents a more complicated problem. Twice Khāravela went to Magadha. In the 8th year he stormed the fortress of Gorathagirī, lying a few miles to the west of Rājagṛha, the ancient capital of Magadha,

---

1. It is significant that the obliteration at the beginning of L 17 is sufficient to contain *Pānatariya-panatisata-vasa* (= The year 355), (ref. p. 22 fn. 1, *supra*).

but did not go further north or east. The term *Rājagṛha-nṛpa* used in this context appears to be synonymous with the 'King of Magadha', whose name was not mentioned here since no direct contact took place with him at that time. This time Khāravela perhaps had no intention of waging a war against Magadha, and the fortress was stormed most probably as a part of strategy for securing his communications in his onward march to Mathura. But the next time, in his twelfth year, he marched into Magadha and then he came into direct contact with its king, Bahasatimitaṁ, whom he made to bow down at his feet.

Literary traditions are silent about any Bahasatimita (Bṛhaspatimitra). Numismatic evidence shows that there was a king of this name about that time. Cast coins bearing the legend 'Bahasatimitasa' have been discovered at Kosam, the site of Kauśāmbī.[1] The script is Aśokan Brāhmī and is supposed to be of the same style as that of an inscription found at Mora in the Mathura district which also mentions 'Bṛhasvāṭimitra'.[2] On stratigraphic grounds these coins are assigned to *circa* 185-115 BC.[3] Struck coins of Bahasatimita have also been found at Kosam and they are also assigned to second century BC.[4] Their palaeography is said to be similar to that of the Pabhosa Cave inscriptions which also mention 'Bahasatimitra'.[5]

This evidence put together indicates that there was a king named Bahasatimita in eastern India in the first quarter of the second century BC, his dominions extended as far as the Vatsa region,[6] his mother Gopālī was the daughter of King Tevaṇiputra

1. Jagannath in *A Comprehensive History of India*, II, p. 107.
2. *J.R.A.S.*, 1912, p. 120.
3. Sharma, G.R., *The Excavations at Kauśāmbī (1957-59)*, pp.19, 80-85.
4. Jagannath, *op. cit.*; also, Allan, J., *British Museum Catalogue of Coins of Ancient India*, p. xcviii.
5. *E.I.*, II, pp. 240-43.
6. The problem of dismemberment of the Maurya Empire has been discussed in detail in my *Political and Cultural History of Mid-North India*.

Bhāgavata of Ahicchatrā, and his daughter Yaśamātā lived at Mathura. King Tevaṇiputra Bhāgavata was the son of King Śonakāyanaputra Vaṁgapāla who appears to have founded his independent kingdom in Ahicchatrā in similar circumstances as did Simuka and Khāravela's grandfather but about two decades later on the death of Samprati. If so, Tevaṇiputra Bhāgavata's daughter's son could be a contemporary of Khāravela and could be his adversary in his twelfth year in *c.* 173 BC.

The instant inscription makes Bahasatimita the king of Magadha and it also seems to indicate that his territory included Aṅga to the east. An examination of the evidence afforded by the *Yugapurāṇa* of the *Gārgī-saṁhitā* and its correlation with the information supplied by the Pabhosa Cave Inscriptions, also suggest that the Maurya dynasty in Magadha was put to an end by the confederacy of the newly formed kingdoms of Mathura and Ahicchatrā and that Bahasatimita who was a prince of the Mathura house but was also the daughter's son of the then King of Ahicchatrā, was installed as King of Magadha in *c.* 206 BC under the regency of an Ahicchatrā prince.[1]

It is believed that in *c.* 187 BC. Bṛhadratha, the last of the Mauryas, was killed by Puṣymitra Śuṅga in Magadha and the latter founded the Śuṅga dynasty. On this account K.P. Jayaswal identified Bahasatimita with Puṣyamitra Śuṅga, saying that Puṣya was a star in the Bṛhaspati constellation. This identification has, however, not been accepted. It is to be noted that no coins of Puṣyamitra Śuṅga have been discovered at least in

1. The tradition contained in the *Yugapurāṇa* seems to suggest that the confederate forces of the Yavanas, Pañcālas and Māthuras put an end to the Maurya rule in Magadha (ref. D.R. Mankad, 'A critically edited text of the Yugapurāṇa', *J.U.P.H.S.,* XX, pp. 32-64). These Yavanas are, however, not to be confused with the hordes of Demetrius because till *c.* 200 BC the Seleucids were still strong and Bactria was yet a satrapy. They could at best be the mercenaries employed by the kings of Mathura and Ahicchatrā.

   The problem of Bahasatimita has been examined at length in my work cited above.

Magadha. No inscription of his or referring to him, has also been found in Magadha. In fact, no Śuṅga inscription has been found in that region.

On one point the Jain and the Brahmanical puranic traditions converge that Puṣyamitra came after the Mauryas. According to the former he ruled for 30 or 35 years and according to the latter, for 36 years. The Jain traditions relate to Ujjayinī. The puranic traditions cannot be definitely located. The story of the *Mālvikāgnimitra*[1] suggests that the headquarters of the *Senāpati* (=Puṣyamitra Śuṅga) were at Vidisha, and those of the *Saciva*, in Vidarbha. This indicates that the event should relate to the Ujjayinī branch of the Mauryas. On epigraphic evidence the eastern-most limit of the Śuṅga dominions appears to be Bharhut,[2] near Nagod in the Satna district. Possibly the dominions of the Śuṅgas, and at least of Puṣyamitra, included only Malwa (Ujjayinī and Vidisha) and Bundelkhand regions in central India. The mere finding of an inscription of Dhana who claims to be the sixth in descent from *Senāpati* Puṣyamitra, at Ayodhya is no conclusive evidence of Puṣyamitra's sway in that region, more so since it does not mention that the findspot was included in his or in the Śuṅga dominions. He had an encounter with the Greeks but that took place on the Kali Sindh in central India; this also lends support to the above view. According to the Jain tradition, Puṣyamitra should have ruled in Ujjayinī from 204 to 174 or 169 BC. The lower limit of his reign appears to be 169 BC since it would be in accord with the puranic tradition assigning him a reign of 36 years. The encounter with the Greeks appears to have taken place towards the close of his reign in view of two facts, firstly that his forces were commanded by his grandson Vasumitra[3] and secondly that according to Justin,

1. A play in classical Sanskrit by Kālidāsa.
2. Dhanabhūti's record on the eastern gateway mentions *Suganaṁ raje* ('in the kingdom of the Śuṅgas'). (Majumdar, N.G., *A Guide to the Sculptures in the Indian Museum*, I, p. 95.)
3. *Vide, Mālavikāgnimitra*.

Demetrius is placed in *c.* 171-136 BC.[1] Khāravela does not mention him as he did not come into any contact with him in the course of any of his campaigns. The above discussion leads us to the conclusion that although Puṣyamitra Śuṅga was also a contemporary of Khāravela, he was different from Bahasatimita of Magadha.

Thus, it is possible to deduce that Khāravela should have ruled in Kaliṅga from *c.* 185 BC to *c.* 172 BC and that since our record does not record any event after the thirteenth year of his reign, it should have been inscribed in *c.* 172 BC.

1. Justin says that Demetrius was 'king of Indians' when Eucratides was the king of Bactria and Mithridates was that of Parthia. The last named is placed in *c.* 171-136 BC.

3

Khāravela

Personal History

THE readings and constructions leave little scope for speculation about the lineage of Khāravela, yet attempts have been made to find references to the puranic Aiḷa, Cedi, Veṇa and Vasū in the inscription. It has also been said that he belonged to the third dynasty of Kaliṅga.

The passage *tatiye-Kaliṁga-rājavaṁse-purisa-yuge* clearly indicates that he was the third in descent in the royal family of Kaliṅga. *Purisa-yuga* = *puruṣa-yuga*, means 'generation',[1] and the governing *tatiye* settles that his was the third generation. He does not mention the names of his father and grandfather, and otherwise also we do not know anything about them, except the inference from this very passage that the grandfather founded the line in Kaliṅga.

The name Khāravela has been mentioned thrice in the inscription: in L 1, L 14 and L 17. At all the three places it is preceded by appropriate titles and epithets, as was the custom. The construction suggests that *Airena* (= *Āryena* = by the high-

1. The term occurs in the *Sukhabodhā* commentary by Devendragaṇin on the *Uttarajhayaṇa Sutta* while describing the episode of the breaking down of nine spokes of Candragupta's chariot as the Nanda's daughter stepped into it. Cāṇakya dispelled Candragupta's fear of a bad omen by saying that it signified that his dynasty would last nine generations (*Nava-purisa-jugāṇi tujjhaṁ vaṁsaṁ holi*). Hemacandra also uses *puruṣa-yugāṇi* in the same sense in the *Pariśiṣṭaparvan* (VIII, v. 326). Both these sources are Jain.

born, noble, honourable) is a mere honorific and its equation with *Aiḷena*, *i.e.*, 'descendent of Iḷa or Iḷā, father or mother of the Purūravas', is not possible. A royal honorific was necessary at the beginning of the description of the king and this purpose could not be served by *Aiḷa*. *Ārya* has been used in the meaning of 'noble, honourable, high-born' in ancient literature usually and it was also the usual form of address in the sense of 'Sir, My Lord, Your Majesty'. The word has no pretensions to the Aryan race, the way it has been used in literature.

If we leave out the epithets, the name complete with honorifics and titles would be 'Ārya Mahārāja Mahāmeghavāhana Kaliṅgādhipati Śrī Khāravela' in L 1, 'Śrī Khāravela' in L 14 and 'Rājā Śrī Khāravela' in L 17. *Mahāmeghavāhana* (lit. Indra, or 'the rider of elephant') appears to be a royal title of the kings of Kaliṅga which they assumed or earned due to the preponderance of elephants in that region. The same honorifics and titles as Khāravela's in L 1 are borne by Kūdepa whose inscription has been found in the nearby Pātālapura cave.[1]

Khāravela is the proper name. It can be equated with Sanskrit *Kṣāra-vella*, meaning 'moving sharp as the wind' or 'the very cyclone'. His career as depicted in this epigraph is true to his name.

He mentions the name of his family as *Cedi-rāja-vaṁsa* which signifies that it originally belonged to the Cedi region. There is no indication for connecting it with the puranic Cedis. As already observed, the founder hailed from the Cedi (Bundelkhand) region, was posted in Kaliṅga, and took advantage of the weakness of the Maurya authority like Simuka who was posted near Nasik. Such migrations were always possible.

The passage *vadhamāna-sesa-yovanābhivijayo* in L 2 simply means 'to make the remainder of his youth (*śeṣa yauvana*)

1. *Airasa Mahārājasa Kaliṁgādhipatino Māhā(megha)vāha(na)sa Kūdepa-sīrino leṇaṁ*. (*I.H.Q.*, XIV, 1, p. 160).

prosperous (*vardhamāna*) by conquests (*abhivijayo*), and there is apparently no allusion to Veṇa or his son Pṛthu. It also appears from the instant record that Khāravela never lost sight of this objective and almost every alternate year he led a campaign of conquest.

The passage *Rājasi-vaṁsa-kula-viniśito* in L 17 also does not contain any reference to the puranic king Rājarṣi Vasū. This epithet describes Khāravela as the 'Support or Refuge of the princely houses and families', and there is nothing unusual in it when we know of his successful expeditions against several princely houses and families.

By its very nature the record is very personal and the author does not mention even the names of any of his predecessors. The possibility of mentioning any legendary heroes is thus precluded. Literal meanings convey reasonable sense and there is no need or scope for assuming references.

An issue was born to him in the seventh regnal year. His name is not mentioned in this epigraph. The Mañcapurī cave, in front and to the south-east of Hāthīgumphā, contains three inscriptions respectively in the upper storey (Svargapurī), lower storey (Pātālapura) and a side wing of the lower storey (Yamapura), recording the dedications of the Agamahisi (Chief Queen) of Kaliṅga-Cakravarti Śrī Khāravela,[1] of Ārya Mahārāja Kaliṅgādhipati Mahāmeghavāhana Śrī Kūdepa, and of Kumāra Vaḍukha.[2] This cave appears to have been reserved exclusively for the members of the royal family. The issue born in the seventh year might be either Vaḍukha or Kūdepa, and it is also possible that Vaḍukha might be his childhood name and Kūdepa, the proper name which he assumed on his succession. Such instances are not unusual.

Khāravela had at least two wives, namely, Vajiragharavatī

---

1. *Arahaṁta-pasādāṁ Kāliṁgānaṁ-Samanānaṁ-leṇaṁ kārito* (,) *Rājino Lalākasa Hathis*(ī)*ha-saṁpanātasa dhutunā Kaliga-Ca(kavatino Siri-Khāra)velasa Agamahisinā kāritaṁ*. (*Ibid.*, p. 159).

2. *Kumāro-Vaḍukhasa leṇaṁ*. (*Ibid.*, p. 161).

who bore him a child in the seventh year (L 7) and Queen Sindhulā of Siṁhapatha (L 15). Since the latter is mentioned with the title of Queen, she appears to be identical with Agamahisi of the Svargapurī record. The location of Svargapurī is in accord with the description of Sindhulā's shrine given in our inscription and this seems to confirm the identification. We thus gather that the Chief Queen of Khāravela was named Sindhulā, she hailed from Siṁhapatha, she was the daughter of King Lalāka Hathisīha, and she followed the religion of her husband. Khāravela refers to her dedication of a shrine, which appears to be confirmed by her own Svargapurī record wherein she is said to have built *Arahaṁta-prāsādaṁ*, *i.e.*, a shrine in the honour of *Arahaṁta* for worship-purpose, as well as *leṇaṁ*, *i.e.*, cave-dwelling for *Śramaṇa*s (ascetics).[1]

The opening of the epigraph with the Jain hymn of obeisance, makes its author definitely a follower of Jainism. It is also confirmed by the fact that the dates mentioned are in M.E., as we have seen above. He calls himself *pūjānurata-uvāsaga*, *i.e.*, 'a lay devotee addicted to worship'. The four-fold Jain congregation consists of monks, nuns, male lay devotees and female lay devotees, and his description of himself is thus in accord with the traditional concept. The description of the assembly is also essentially Jain.

But he was not intolerant or fanatic. Nowhere does he disparage, criticise or show disrespect to other religions. In fact, he takes pride in calling himself as *Sava-pāsaṁḍa-pūjako* (worshipper of all sects) and *sava-devāyatana-saṁkhārakārako* (embellisher of all temples) (L 17); and at the *Savagahanaṁ* ceremony in Mathura he worshipped the *Arahaṁta* and at the same time gave gifts to the Brahmins (L 9). This catholicity of

1. The terms *Arahaṁta* and *Śramaṇa* have distinct connotation. *Arahaṁta* is the reverenced (*pūjya*) deity who has cast off transmigration and is no longer a mortal; *Śramaṇa* is a revered recluse or ascetic who is a mortal like us but deserves respect for going homeless in pursuit of spiritual attainment. B.M. Barua confused the two terms in his translation cited on p. 31 *supra*.

outlook and broad liberalism was the characteristic trait of nearly all the successful Indian rulers. It is also a fact that all his expeditions were purely political and military campaigns and none of them was guided by any religious motive. N.K. Sahu's suggestion that Khāravela was a Jain by birth, *i.e.*, Jainism was his family religion,[1] appears to be acceptable.

Considerable care appears to have been bestowed upon his education. He was given training not only in Correspondence,[2] Currency,[3] Accountancy,[4] State Regulations and Laws,[5] but was also taught music and was given a liberal education covering other sciences, so as to make him an accomplished and cultivated king. He was associated with administration at the age of fifteen when he was made the Yuvarāja (Crown Prince) and for full nine years he was given practical training in administration. No epigraphic record of such meticulous training of a prince has so far come to light.

At the age of twenty-four he became the king. Being a *yuvarāja* already, there would not have been any difficulty in succession. The word *pāpunāti* seems to suggest some trouble, but the context does not support such a suggestion and it appears

1. *A History of Orissa*, ed. N.K. Sahu, (1st edn., 1956, Susil Gupta), vol. II, p. 329.
2. *Lekha* stands for official correspondence. Kauṭilya has dealt with the subject at considerable length (*Arthaśāstra*, trans. R. Shamasastry, 4th edn., pp. 71-75). A manual named *Lekha-paddhati* was also written in the time of the Cālukyas of Anahilapāṭana.
3. Buddhaghosa, (*S.B.E.*, XIII, p. 201), and Kauṭilya, (*op. cit.*, p. 95), have also used *rūpa* in the sense of coins or currency. It broadly covers the science dealing with public finance.
4. *Gaṇanā* stands for accountancy and broadly covers the science dealing with public accounts.
5. *Vavahāra* and *Vidhi* stand for laws. *Vavahāra* (= *vyavahāra*) stands for the law as defined by practice and seems to cover the mass of precedents, State Regulations and customary laws.

   Vidhi denotes the positive injunctions — the laws as they were.

   For effective dispensation of justice, knowledge of both the Code and the Regulations (which supplement the former) is essential.

to be a matter of style only. The event of his father's death has been ignored altogether, most probably because the record is too personal. Our record closes in his thirteenth regnal year when he was only 37 years old. Nothing is known about him after that year.

Campaigns

He led six campaigns in all, one in the second year, one in the fourth year, one in the eighth year, one in the eleventh year and two in the twelfth year. They appear to be merely campaigns of conquest and no annexations appear to have been made except in one case. They, however, help in determining the extent of Khāravela's Kaliṅga.

The first campaign was in the western direction up to the capital of the Asikas on the R. Kaṁhabeṁā (Kr̥ṣṇaveṇā). The direction suggests that the Kr̥ṣṇvenā should be identified with the Wainganga.[1] Its identification with the Krishna which flows to the south of Kaliṅga and not to the west, is incorrect. It is not possible to locate Asikanagara which probably lay across the Wainganga. In fact, his army reached only the river and does not appear to have sacked or entered the town itself. Presence and manoeuvres of his army on his side of the river were sufficient to cause alarm to the people across the river. The object of the campaign appears to be exploratory in the main and it seems to indicate that the Wainganga formed the western boundary of the kingdom of Kaliṅga.

The next expedition, in the fourth year, was a campaign of conquest. It was also in the western direction and was personally

---

1. It joins the Pranhita at Seoni, which, in its turn, joins the Godavari near Sironcha, both in the Chandrapur district, Maharashtra.

   Barua supports this identification on the ground that the main tributary of the Wainganga is the Kanhan which joins it in the Bhandara district (*I.H.Q.*, XIV, 3, p. 475 fn. 166), suggesting thereby that it might be known as Kanha-Wainā or Kr̥ṣṇā-veṇā. I am inclined to agree with him.

led by him. He crossed into the Vindhyas[1] and defeated the Raṭhikas and Bhojakas. These Raṭhikas and Bhojakas bore all the insignia of royalty, namely, crown, caparisoned horse, umbrella and golden pitcher. In the inscriptions of Aśoka the Riṣṭikas and Bhojas are listed among the *aparātās* or the people living in western India. They appear to have been autonomous tribes under the protectorate of the Maurya Empire. The Sātavāhanas coveted their friendship and did not interfere with them. Queen Nāgānikā was the daughter of a Mahāraṭhi. They seem to have been knit together in a loose confederation, enjoying all the rights and prerogatives of sovereignty, and in alliance with the Sātavāhanas. Their territories seem to be interspersed in the central and western Deccan in the hilly tracts and lay between Kaliṅga and Nasik. Their confederate forces appear to have been defeated by Khāravela. It is, however, not known where the battle was actually fought. The battle was decisive and his western flank was fully secured as we do not hear of any further expedition in that direction. As the context shows, it should have been fought somewhere in the Vindhyas, not very far from Kaliṅga, across the Wainganga and below the Narmada. There does not appear to be any exaggeration in his statement that the former kings of Kaliṅga did not go as far as the Vindhyas, and he also did not cross the Vindhyas into Malwa so as to come into contact with the Śuṅgas, or go very deep into the Vindhyas westward so as to come into direct contact with the Sātavāhanas. No annexations are claimed; he was satisfied by making his adversaries submit to him and by seizing their jewels and fortune.

The third expedition, in the eighth year, is northward. He

---

1. The Vindhyas have been referred to in the inscription as *Vijādharādhivāsaṁ* (*Vidyādhara + adhivāsaṁ*) poetically. In the Jain puranic lore these ranges are generally referred to as the abode of the Vidyādharas.

   Jagannath's suggestion that it refers to some sacred place of the Jains and its violation by the Raṭhikas and Bhojakas was the immediate cause of war, (*op. cit.*, pp. 113-14), is not acceptable in the context. It is a geographical term pure and simple.

first mentions the storming of Gorathagiri, near Rājagr̥ha. It seems to indicate that to the north the boundaries of Kaliṅga were nearly contiguous with those of Magadha. Gorathagiri was a hill fortress, serving as a defence for Rājagr̥ha, the ancient capital of Magadha, and it lay in the Barabar Hills, some six miles to the west of Vaibhar Hill in Rajgir in the Nalanda district of south Bihar. Its situation in the southern part of Magadha suggests the contiguity of the southern boundaries of Magadha and the northern boundaries of Kaliṅga. Khāravela did not go further into Magadha and seems to have turned westward to Mathura. The storming of this fortress was merely a strategic measure to secure his communications in the rear in his onward march.

Since he claims to have reached the Yamuna river after liberating the city of Mathura, he appears to have marched through the tract lying below the Ganga and Yamuna. It was not intractable. A battle appears to have been fought near Mathura. It is suggested by *vipamuñcitu* (having liberated). But the name of the adversary, who appears to have been an aggressor, is not mentioned. It has been sought to read *Yavana-rāja Dimita* and to identify him with Demetrius. In the note on the text it has already been indicated that this reading is highly doubtful and the reading more appropriately appears to be *Yamanā-nadīṁ*. The event took place in *c.* 178 BC and if Justin is to be believed, Demetrius should have come at least seven years later. It may be that there was some depredation from the north or from any of the neighbouring kingdoms and Mathura was temporarily occupied by the aggressor, and Khāravela drove out the aggressor and restored Mathura to its legitimate ruler.[1] It was a mere act of chivalry. Mathura was not annexed, and therefore on liberation it should have been

1. If the *Yuga-Purāṇa* tradition carries any historical background, there is a strong suggesion that the Greek mercenaries who followed in the train of the confederate armies of Mathura and Ahicchatrā to Pāṭaliputra, turned hostile and on their way back, seized Mathura itself either to claim their dues or to satiate their greed for plunder or both. In all probability, Khāravela had liberated Mathura from these Greek mercenaries turned hostile.

returned to its rightful owner. His further activities in Mathura were confined to performing religious ceremonies.

The real campaigns of conquest were yet to follow, and preparations for these were made in the tenth year. For the next two years he remained busy in these campaigns, marching to the south, then to the north, and again to the south. His ambition was to conquer the whole country and live up to the ideal of a *Cakravartin*.[1] This is the earliest epigraphic record mentioning the name of the country as Bhāratavarṣa (*Bharadavasa*).[2]

Having made the necessary preparations in the tenth year, he first marches to the south, in the eleventh year, and sacks Pithuṇḍa, the metropolis of Ava kings. Pithuṇḍa can be identified with Pityndra, mentioned by Ptolemy as the metropolis of Maisolia and the Arvarnoi.[3] It lay in the interior of Maisolia, the coast between the rivers Godavari and Krishna. It has been suggested that possibly it did not lie very far from Vijayapurī (of the Nagarjunikonda Inscription), Amaravati and Vijayawada, in the heart of ancient Āndhrapatha.[4] Exact location is not

---

1. *i.e.*, supreme over-lord. This ideal is common to all the Indian traditions. According to the Jain tradition, there have been 12 *Cakravartins* who had conquered the whole earth, and the first among them was Bharata, the son of Ṛṣabha, the first *Tīrthaṅkara*. (See *Mahāpurāṇam*, *Triśaṣṭiśalākāpuruṣacarita*).

2. In the Jain tradition Bharata, the son of Ṛṣabha, is credited with giving the country this name, while in the Brahmanical tradition Bharata, the son of Duṣyanta and Śakuntalā immortalised in the *Abhijñāna-Śākuntalam* of Kālidāsa, is also credited with it.

   Thus, in essence, both the Jain and Brahmanical traditions are unanimous as regards the name *Bhāratavarṣa* for the geographical entity now known as *India*. However, the Buddhist tradition calls it *Jambūdīpa*, and in his M.R.E. I Aśoka mentions *Jambūdīpa* in that sense — perhaps the only epigraphic mention known so far.

3. *Ptolemy's Ancient India*, ed. by S.N. Majumdar, pp. 67-68, 185.

4. H.C. Raychaudhuri in *The Early History of the Deccan*, Pt. I-VI, p. 56. It is also identified with Pihuṇḍa mentioned in the *Uttarādhyayanasūtra*, which, however, does not help in locating it.

known. The Arvarnoi of Ptolemy may be identical with the Ava people, or else *Ava* is a misreading for *Aṁdha*, meaning the Āndhra kings in the context, which is not quite impossible.

The southern boundary of Kaliṅga appears to be the Godavari. The manner in which Khāravela marches to Pithuṇḍa, shows that it could not be very far from Kaliṅga and must be somewhere near the southern border across the Godavari. The way in which it was sacked, seems to indicate that the Pithuṇḍa kingdom was annexed and the southern boundary was extended as far as the Krishna. Khāravela was now face to face with the Tamila Confederacy which he set out to break 'for the well-being of his realm'. He claims to have broken the Confederacy, but does not mention to have marched further south and it indicates that the Confederacy was broken through diplomacy rather than warfare. The Colas[1] were probably the northern-most member of the Confederacy, whose territory lay between the Pithuṇḍa and the Pāṇḍya kingdoms. They seem to have been won over and he was thus enabled to march forth to the Pāṇḍya kingdom the following year.

In the twelfth year he led two expeditions: one to the north and the other to the south. He marched forth into Magadha up to the Ganga[2] and obtained the submission of the Magadha king Bahasatimita. Although the name of Pāṭaliputra is not mentioned the reference is evidently to that city which lay on the Ganga, and had continued to be the capital of Magadha at least since the days of the Nandas. The fact that he worshipped

1. Aśoka mentions the Pāṇḍyas after the Colas. The Pāṇḍyas have also been associated with Madurai on the R. Vaigai from very ancient times, while the Colas have been associated with Thanjavur on the R. Kaveri, which lies to the north of Madurai.
2. The reading is *hathasaṁ Gaṁgāya pāyayati*, *i.e.*, he makes his elephants and horses (*hathasaṁ = hasti + aśvam*) drink in the Ganga. There is no reference to the Sugāṅgīya palace, as supposed by Jayaswal and Banerji (*E.I.*, XX, p. 88 fn. 8). This name of the palace of Candragupta Maurya is mentioned only in a very late work of fiction, the *Mudrārākṣasa*, and it is not mentioned in any of the traditional accounts or epigraphic records.

in the temple which enshrined the image taken away by the Nanda king from Kaliṅga, seems to indicate it.

He simply claims to have struck terror into the hearts of the kings of Uttarāpatha (*Utarāpadha*), which means that he did not come into contact with any other king of north India and did not go beyond Magadha. Here Uttarāpatha has been used in the common sense of the term, meaning North India. Two broad divisions of the country have been Uttarāpatha and Dakṣiṇāpatha, the former referring to the region lying to the north of the Vindhyas and the latter, to that lying to the south of the Vindhyas.[1] An inference to the north-western region beyond Pṛthudaka (near Thanesar), cannot be drawn from Uttarāpatha here as the context does not at all support it.[2]

After the successful expedition against Magadha in the north, he marched against the Pāṇḍyas, perhaps the most powerful member of the Tamila Confederacy, in the south. He calls his victory against the Pāṇḍyas 'a portentous marvel',[3] and this seems to indicate the power of the Pāṇḍyas. The operation against the Pāṇḍyas appears to have been two-fold, *i.e.*, military as well as naval. Elephants formed the task-force on land and boats were used on the sea. This is the earliest epigraphic reference to the use of boats for war purposes, and it seems to

1. More correctly the dividing line is the R. Narmada.
2. Jagannath (*op. cit.*, p. 114, fn.3), also takes it to have been used in a general way for North India. *Uttarāpatha* finds the earliest epigraphic mention here.

   A seminar was held at Bhubaneshwar on January 16-18, 1999, at a stupendous cost of Rs. 7 lakh, they say, to put scholars' seal on Acharya Vidyanandji's highly imaginative discovery that Khāravela went on campaign to Takṣaśilā (Taxila in Rawalpindi district, Pakistan) on the basis of the mention of *Utarāpadha* in his inscription. And, *adbhutam āsacaryam* it was that by spending Rs. 37000 per scholar, as they say, strenuous publicity could be given to this myth to overshadow history.
3. *Abhutamachariyaṁ* = *adbhutam* + *āścaryam*, or *abhūtam* + *āścaryam*. In both the cases the meaning remains the same.

confirm the overseas activities of the Kaliṅga people.[1] Khāravela is, however, not known to have led any overseas expedition although he maintained a fleet of war-ships.

Dominions

The kingdom of Kaliṅga as inherited by Khāravela appears to have comprised the entire territory known as Tri-Kaliṅga, including Utkala, Tosala and Kaliṅga.[2] It was bounded on the north by the R. Ḍamodara, beyond which lay Magadha; on the west by the R. Wainganga, beyond which lived the Asikas and the Raṭhikas and Bhojakas; on the south by the R. Godavari, beyond which lay the Pithuṇḍa kingdom and the Tamila countries; and on the east by the Bay of Bengal. Khāravela appears to have annexed the Pithuṇḍa kingdom. The total annihilation of Pithuṇḍa signified by its being ploughed by ploughs drawn by asses, seems to suggest annexation. The boundaries were thus extended up to the R. Krishna in the south. All other expeditions of his were aimed at obtaining formal submission and allegiance so as to secure his frontiers.

The capital of Kaliṅga (*Kaliṁga-nagarī*) should lie somewhere on the R. Prachi on both banks of which Khāravela built the Mahāvijayaprāsāda. It should not be very far from the sea coast since it is stated to have been ravaged by a cyclone. The name of the city does not appear to have been mentioned. *Khibīraṁ* is merely its adjective, meaning 'the Abode of the Brave' (*Kṣi*: dim. of *kṣiti*: + *vīram*). It appears to have been a

1. See Mazumdar, B.C., *Orissa in the Making*, and Gerini, *Researches on Ptolemy*, pp. 119-39. "Kaliṅga had built up a great overseas empire and spread her colonies as far as Philippine islands in the east and far south into the islands of the Indian Archipelago" (Sahu, N.K., ed., *A History of Orissa*, vol. I, p. 62).

2. Utkala lay between the rivers Daṃodar and Brahmani, Uttara Tosala between the Brahmani and the Mahanadi, Dakṣiṇa Tosala or Koṅgoda between the Mahanadi and the Vansadhara, and Kaliṅga between the Vansadhara and the Godavari (*vide*, Banerji, R.D., *History of Orissa*, vol. I, map opp. p. 49).

custom in Kaliṅga and the neighbouring region to name the capital after the name of the people, region or kingdom, *e.g.*, the capital of the Asikas was called Asikanagara, the principal city in the Tosala region was called Tosali, and similarly the capital of the Kaliṅga kingdom was called Kaliṅganagarī.

It has been sought to identify it with either Dhauli or Śiśupālagarh.[1] Dhauli lies in the Puri district, on the metalled road from Cuttack to Puri, a little distant from the R. Prachi. A set of Aśoka's Rock Edicts, including the Kaliṅga Edicts addressed to the Mahāmātras of Tosali and Samāpā, has been found inscribed on a low hill there and near that there is an open stretch of land of ancient habitation extending up to the river. It represents the site of Tosali since *Tosali* can be phonetically corrupted into *Dhauli*, and also because it lies in the Tosala region which covered the Mahanadi delta and extended up to the R. Vansadhara to the south. It is possible that Khāravela's grandfather was the Mahāmātra of Tosali. There seems to be strong indication that Tosali was not adopted as the capital of the newly founded kingdom, but a site nearby, which was just on the banks of the river, was chosen for the new capital. The exact location of the Tansauliyavāṭā canal is not known, but the context seems to suggest that it was brought into the capital from a nearby place, most probably from the old town of Tosali into the new capital.

Śiśupālagarh lies 1½ miles east-southwest of Bhubaneshwar and six miles to its west-northwest are the Khaṇḍagiri-Udayagiri hills. According to B.B. Lal, a presumption is raised in favour of its being identical with Khāravela's Kaliṅganagarī on the following pieces of circumstantial evidence: no fortified town of comparable date except Śiśupālagarh is known to exist near about the Khaṇḍagiri-Udayagiri hills, and the excavations did reveal a collapse and subsequent repair of the southern gateway-flank of the fortifications which seems to confirm

1. The suggestion that it might be Kalingapatnam in the Srikakulam district (*E.I.*, XX, p. 83 fn. 19), is not worth considering since it does not answer to the description given in the inscription.

Khāravela's statement that he got repaired the gateway and fortification-wall which had been damaged by a storm.[1] The upper limit of the site is placed at *c*. 300 BC, its Early Period being 300-200 BC, Early Middle Period 200 BC-AD 100, Late Middle Period AD 100-200 and Late Period AD 200-350. It is difficult to support this presumption in view of the fact that Kaliṅganagarī must be on the Prachi and Śiśupālagarh does not fulfil that condition. Its proximity with the Khaṇḍagiri-Udayagiri is not so relevant in the context. The fortress may have served the same defence purposes for the old town of Tosali as well as the new capital, as were served by Gorathagiri for Rājagṛha.

The new capital was a walled town, with gateways having pinnacles on which were flown the royal banners. It had cool reservoir and parks. It probably suffered from scarcity of water and so Khāravela brought the Tanasuliyavāṭā canal into it. He also added to its beauty by building the Mahāvijayaprāsāda on both banks of the Prachi river at a cost of 38 lakhs.[2] The two portions of the palace appear to have been linked through bridges. It should have been a beautiful thing and a marvel of engineering for those times but in the absence of any physical remains, as also any reference in literature, it is not possible to catch a glimpse of it.

1. 'An early historical fort in Eastern India', *Ancient India*, No. 5, (January 1949), pp. 66-67.
2. The plural ending of *sahasehi* (*sahasrāni*) clearly points to the cost as 'thirty-eight hundred thousands'. There is, however, no information as to the name or value of the standard in which this amount has been denoted. The finding of a silver punch-marked coin from the filling forming the terrace in front of the Hāthīgumphā (*I.A.R.*, 1961-62, p. 37), might suggest that the costs were mentioned in terms of silver coin current in those days.

4

Socio-Political Conditions

LITERARY prescriptions about the education, training and accomplishments of princes in ancient India are amply confirmed by this epigraph. Sports, Correspondence, Currency, Accountancy, State Regulations and Laws, Music, Diplomacy and War, appear to have been the compulsory subjects of study. General education was also imparted to cover other subjects. Practical training in administration was also imparted through active association before the reins of government were actually handed over.

The two objects of kings appear to have been to make conquests and to make their subjects happy. The numerous literary references to the duties of kings are hereby confirmed through epigraphic evidence.

The traditional four-fold division of army into cavalry, elephants, infantry and chariots, was in vogue. Navy was also maintained by the coastal kingdoms.

Crown, caparisoned horse, umbrella and golden pitcher[1] were the accepted insignia of royalty, and the kings were believed to possess auspicious marks.

---

1. These have been mentioned in connection with the Raṭhikas and Bhojakas. *Makuṭa* (*mukuṭa*) is crown, *chata* (*chatra*) is umbrella, and *bhiṁgāra* (*bhṛṅgāra*) is golden pitcher. *Sabiladhite* seems to stand for 'caparisoned horse'. *Bila* means Indra's horse Ucchaiḥśravas in particular, and horse in general. With *sa* (= *su* = well) and *dhite* (= *dhṛte* = maintained), it would mean 'well maintained horse', and in the context it may be translated as 'caparisoned horse'.

Works of public welfare were executed by the state. At least two irrigation projects of ancient India are definitely known: the Tanasuliyavāṭā canal in Kaliṅga and the Sudarśana lake in Saurāṣṭra. The former was carved out by the Nanda kiṅg (in 424 BC) and extended by Khāravela 244 years later (in *c.* 180 BC), while the latter was executed by Candragupta Maurya (in 312 BC), about 127 years prior to Khāravela, in west India and it has a recorded history of additions and alterations by successive rulers for about 700 years. We do not know anything about the Kaliṅga project after Khāravela, yet it has a history of more than 250 years.

Festivals and fairs[1] were organised by the state to entertain the people. Performances of folk dances, classical dances, songs and instrumental music[2] were also organised.

It also appears to have been customary to show off royal opulence[3] and on that occasion to remit taxes, bestow grants and sanction other favours to the people. Khāravela did it in his sixth regnal year.

Some distinction between the townsmen and the villagers appears to have subsisted in the matter of taxes, etc. It also

---

1. *Usava* (= *utsava* = festival) and *samāja* (an assemblage for merry-making, *melā*, convivial gathering, fair) have been used in a secular sense. The former was accompanied by public feasting while the latter, by various items of amusement. Numerous references to *samāja* are found in the *Mahābhārata* and the Buddhist literature. Aśoka also refers to it in his R.E. I. From the *Sīgālovādasutta* we learn that *naccaṁ* (dances), *gītaṁ* (songs), *vāditaṁ* (music), *akkhānaṁ* (dramatics), *pānisaraṁ* (cymbals) and *kumbhathūnaṁ* (pitcher-dances), used to take place in the *samājas*.

2. Khāravela mentions the performances of *dapa*, *nata* (*nṛtya*), *gīta* and *vādita*. The last two stand for music, vocal and instrumental respectively. Likewise, the first two stand for dances, folk and classical respectively. The context does not allow the interpretation of *dapa* as acrobatics or combats. All the four should relate to the *gandharva-vidyā*.

3. *rājaseyaṁ* = *rājaśrīyām*.

appears that Kaliṅga in the time of Khāravela contained several towns.

Polygamy was in vogue. The title of *Agamahisi* (*Agramahiṣī*) for one of his queens clearly indicates that Khāravela had more than one wife. The wife who bore children appears to have been given added honour or endearment, as may be inferred from the way in which the event of the seventh year is mentioned. Khāravela endearingly calls her *Gharini* (*Gṛhiṇī*), *i.e.*, 'housewife'.[1]

The ploughing of a metropolis by ploughs drawn by asses appears to have been the sign of complete annihilation of its ruler.[2]

Political alliances in the form of confederacies were in vogue, *e.g.*, the confederacy of the Tamila countries, as also that of the Raṭhikas and Bhojakas.

It was customary to give the Brahmins gifts on ceremonial occasions.

Image-worship was in vogue and temples were built at least in Kaliṅga and Magadha in Khāravela's times.

The land of the Pāṇḍyas was rich in jewels, gems, pearls and rubies. Beryl was known.

No precise information is available as regards the administrative set up under Khāravela. The dedicatory inscriptions in the nearby caves,[3] which are palaeographically

---

1. The alternative reading *Vajiraghara-khatiyā-sati-gharini* would mean 'faithful wife Vajiraghara Kṣatriyā'. In the adopted reading the meaning is 'wife named (*ghusita* — √*ghush*) Vajiragharavati'.

2. According to Haribhadra (*Āvaśyakavṛtti*) and Hemacandra, Kuṇika (Ajātaśatru) also ploughed Vaiśālī with ploughs drawn by asses after defeating the Licchavis. (*J.B.O.R.S.*, XIII, p. 231).

3. See *E.I.*, XIII, and *I.H.Q.*, XIV, 1, pp. 161-66. In these inscriptions *leṇa* has been used in the meaning of cave-dwelling excavated for the residence of the *Śramaṇas*, *pasāda* (*prāsāda*) in that of shrine for worship purposes, and *koṭhājeyā* in that of circumambulatory path around the *pasāda*.

of the same age, seem to contain the names of some of his officers. They are: Nagara-akhadaṁsa Bhūti (Vyāghra-gumphā), Kaṁma Halakhiṇa (Sarpa-gumphā), Cūlakama (Sarpa-gumphā and Pāvana-gumphā), Mahāmada (= Mahāmātra) Bāriyāya Nākiya (Jambeśvara-gumphā), Atasukhapradinaka (Choṭā Hāthīgumphā), and Pādamulika Kusuma (Tattva-gumphā No. II).[1] It appears that at least two classes of officers, *viz.*, Mahāmātra and Nagara-viyohālaka (Nagara-akhadaṁsa) of the Maurya set up continued under the new kingdom of Kaliṅga.

1. All these caves except the last named are on the Udayagiri. The Tattva-gumphā No. II is on the Khaṇḍagiri.

5

Jainism

THE significance which the Bhabru Edict of Aśoka has for Buddhism, the Hāthīgumphā Inscription of Khāravela has for Jainism, perhaps even more since it seems to preserve and confirm traditions and does not merely serve to demostrate that its author was a follower of Jainism.

The *Pañca-namaskāra*, or the Five-fold Obeisance, hymn of the Jains reads:

> *Ṇamo Arahaṁtāṇaṁ, Ṇamo Siddhāṇaṁ, Ṇamo Āiriyāṇaṁ,*
>
> *Ṇamo Uvajjhāyāṇaṁ, Ṇamo loe savva Sāhūṇaṁ.*[1]

Its antiquity is lost into oblivion. It is found in the most ancient Jain literature available, and appears to have had the same significance for the Jains as '*Buddham saraṇam gacchāmi, Dhammam saraṇam gacchāmi, Saṁgham saraṇam gacchāmi*' has had for the Buddhists. Our inscription begins with *Namo Arahaṁtānaṁ Namo sava Sidhānaṁ* and serves as the earliest preserved record for this hymn in its traditional form.

---

1. *Arahaṁta* (who has cast off transmigration), *siddha* (the Released, *i.e.*, the perfect soul in the stage after *nirvāṇa*), *Ācārya* (master of spiritual knowledge), *upādhyāya* (teacher of spiritual knowledge) and *sādhu* (ascetic), are recognised as deserving supreme veneration (*parameṣṭhi*).

   Among the Jains, *arahaṁta* is not the common term for ascetics. The ascetics are called *samaṇa* (*śramaṇa*), *sāhū* (*sādhu*), or, *muni*. It is amply clear from this inscription and the inscriptions in the nearby caves that shrines were built in the honour of the *Arahaṁta*, while cave-dwellings were excavated for the use of the *Śramaṇas*. Also ref. fn. 1 on p. 50 *supra*.

The term *Arahaṁta* has been explained in L 14 and this is also the earliest preserved record of such an explanation. *Arahaṁta* are they who have cast off transmigration (*pakhiṇasaṁsitehi* = Skt. *prakṣipta saṁsṛtāḥ*). Kunda-kunda, reputed to be one of the earliest Jain authors whose works have been handed down to the posterity and assigned to the early part of the first century AD, defines *Arahaṁta* as follows:

Jara-vāhi-jamma-maraṇaṁ ca-u-ga-i-gamaṇaṁ ca puṇṇapāvaṁ ca.

Haṁtūṇa dosakamme huu ṇāṇamayaṁ ca Arahaṁto.[1]

Kunda-kunda appears merely to elucidate what Khāravela has explained.

The Jain congregation is four-fold, consisting of monks, nuns, male lay devotees (*uvāsaga* = Skt. *upāsaka, śrāvaka*) and female lay devotees. The *uvāsaga* should, according to Khāravela, perform the vows and be addicted to worship. Twelve vows are prescribed in the Scripture for the *uvāsaga* or *śrāvaka*, and here again our inscription seems to corroborate the textual lore. The belief that the performance of the prescribed vows makes one resplendent with supernatural powers,[2] was not unnatural.

---

1. *Kunda-kunda Prābhṛta Saṁgraha,* ed. K.C. Shastri, p. 90. It means: The *Arahaṁta* is he who has attained enlightenment, having destroyed the evils of old age, disease, birth, death, transmigration, merit and sin, and the *karmas*.

2. The terms *rāja-bhatinā* (*rāja-bhaktinaḥ*) and *cina-vatānā* (*cīrṇavratānaḥ*), occurring in L 14, help in determining the sense of the following *vasa-sitānā*. Literally it would be *vas* (= grow bright) + *sita* (= white), and in the context it seems to suggest 'resplendent with supernatural powers'.

   Jayaswal and Banerji have inferred offering of China clothes (silks) and white clothes to the monks from *cina-vatāni* and *vāsā-sitāni* (ref. p. 31 *supra*). Silk is made from silk worms and is, therefore, not acceptable to a Jain monk of any denomination. The rhythmic second part would also not thus mean 'white clothes'.

   N.K. Sahu has suggested that Khāravela was the worshipper of the monks who clad in fine cloth (*cinavatānaṁ* = skt. *jhina vāstrāṇām*) →

There is also a reference to duality of soul (*jīva*) and matter (*deha*) in the passage *jīva-deha-siritā*. The Jains recognise two categories as *jīva* (soul) and *ajīva* (non-soul). Soul is independent, with a separate entity altogether, and is not to be identified with the body (*deha*), a form of matter (*pudgala* which is *ajīva*), in which it is contained for the time being. Khāravela's statement that his soul is dependent (*siritā* = Skt. *āśrita*) upon body, is quite in accord with the Jain concept.

He also defines *Śramaṇa* as *suvihita* or self-possessed. *Śramaṇa* is the general term for Jain monks. Kunda-kunda defined a Jain monk in the following terms:

Dehādisaṁgarahio māṇakasāehiṁ sayalaparichatto
Appā appammi rao sa bhāvaliṁgī have sāhū.[1]

It is again an amplification of Khāravela's definition.

The order of the monks appears to have consisted of different grades which are mentioned in a descending order. First come the *Śramaṇa*s who appear to have been quite unconcerned with all mundane affairs, then come the *Jñānī*s who appear to have been masters of the Scripture, next come the *Tapasvī-Ṛṣi*s who appear to have laid more stress on penance, and lastly come the *Saṁghayana*s, or the leaders of the *Saṁgha*s, who by the very nature of their work were concerned with organisational matters more particularly, and therefore were the less detached

---

→ observed the rainy season retreat (*vāsāsitānaṁ*), and surmised, "this probably indicates that Khāravela was an advocate of the Śvetāmbara form of Jainism and the monks of that sect were receiving royal endowment (*rājabhitinaṁ*)", (*vide*, *Khāravela*, pp. 87-88). This surmise is wide off the mark because the sect of the white-robed was yet to formalize (see App. III *infra*).

1. *Op. cit.*, p. 125.

   It means: Only he is an ascetic in reality who does not possess any physical belongings, has completely cast off ego or pride, and is totally absorbed in his self (soul, *appā* = *ātmā*).

from mundane affairs as compared to the other three.[1] This is the earliest recorded evidence of the existence of different *Saṁgha*s of the Jain monks.

In his thirteenth regnal year in *c*. 172 BC Khāravela convened a Council of Jain monks. No mention of it is found in the literature of either the Digambara or the Śvetāmbara sect of the Jains possibly because it relates to a period till when the schism had not been finalised and the main object of its meeting was to avert the schism and attempt reconciliation. Since it was not palatable to the later protagonists of the two sects they thought it better to ignore and forget it. While disagreeing on the fundamentals, they seem to have agreed on this piece of practical wisdom. There was a school in Mathura which tried to keep away from schismatic tendencies till the first few centuries of the Christian era, and it might have preserved the memory of this Council, but no literature of this school has come to light. It seems to have been represented by the *Ārātiya yati*s or the *Yāpaniya*s.[2]

The Council met on the Mt. Kumārī (the Udayagiri hill, the findspot of the instant record near Bhubaneshwar), which was

1. The *Saṁghayana* of the record recalls the *Ācārya* of the traditional parlance, while *Jñāni* represents the *Upādhyāya* and *Tapasvī-Ṛṣi*, the *Sāhū* (*Sādhu*). The heirachical order given here places *Ācārya* below *Sāhū*, but in the *Pañca-Namaskāra* current now, *Ācārya* has superceded the *Upādhyāya* and *Sāhū*. It was obviously a later manipulation by some ambitious Saṁghayana to invest him with authority and power over both the house-holder and the house-leaving adherents, and since it was a matter of common advantage, leaders of all the Saṁghas acquiesced in it irrespective of doctrinal or denominational differences. The earliest literary mention of the current *ṇamokāra* does not go beyond the close of the 1st century AD among the Digambaras (*vide*, *Ṣaṭkhaṇḍāgama*) and 5th century AD among the Śvetāmbaras (ref. Vallabhī Vācanā).
2. The *Yāpanīya* sect formally came into existence towards the middle of the second century AD. It was a reversion to the austere, and also an effort to bridge up the gap between the Śvetāmbara and Digambara modes and doctrines. It has, all the same, no relation to *yāpujavakehi* in L 14 of our inscription.

somehow considered auspicious[1] and lay in the Vijaya district. It appears to have been a well-attended assembly in which 3500 monks from all directions joined. The site of the assembly was the quadrangle near the shrine of the *Arahaṁta* on the top of the hill. This shrine was on the roof of the Hāthīgumphā on the face of which our record is inscribed. The quadrangle consisted of the stone platform adjacent to the shrine dedicated by Queen Sindhulā. As we have already seen above, Sindhulā's shrine was the upper storey of the Mañcapurī which lies in front and to the south-east of the Hāthīgumphā, and seems to fully fit in the description.

In front of the Assembly Hall was set up a pale-red and quadrilateral pillar inlaid with beryl, apparently to serve as a replica of the *Mānastambha*, in accord with the traditional description of *Samavasaraṇa* (the Preaching Hall of *Tīrthaṅkara*). At the Council the Principal Scripture was given a reading. This is again in accord with the traditional description of Jain Councils as *vācanā* (Reading), found in literature.

The excavations have revealed the remains of an apsidal structure just overlying the Hāthīgumphā. It has an axial length of 78 feet 1 inch and a basal width of 46 feet. It was built of large laterite blocks, 8 courses of which were visible. The circular structure towards the apse might be a *stūpa* or just a round platform on which the object of worship was placed. All this is in perfect accord with what the inscription says about the Relic Memorial (*Kāya-Nisīdīyā*) excavated by Khāravela.

Further, the excavations have also revealed an ancient imposing ramp built of laterite blocks. It is 3 metre wide, rises from the foot of the hill and reaches the terrace of the Hāthīgumphā, and is supported on either side by retaining walls. It is wedge-shaped in plan, showing greater width near the head than at the tail. This ramp seems to represent the quadrilateral pillar mentioned in the inscription.

1. In L 14 *supavata* (*su*[dim. *śubha*] + *parvata*) is an adjective of *Kumārī Pavata* (*Parvata*). The locative endings of *cake* and *pavate* settle the meaning.

At a certain distance from the bottom of the ramp there are two walls at right angles to support the filling below terrace in front of the Hāthīgumphā in sandstone and laterite. The dexter wall is of sandstone and is prominently battered; it is discernible up to the original steps leading to the cave which contains the inscription of the Chief Queen. Carved stone railings and upper part of a female statue in sandstone have been found near the steps. The railings might have embellished Sindhulā's shrine.

The archaeological evidence[1] put together suggests that the shrine over the Hāthīgumphā, the ramp in front of it and the cave to which the dexter wall leads, were the product of a single building activity. It thus confirms the epigraphic evidence as interpreted above about the location of the shrines of Khāravela and Sindhulā as well as of the site for the assembly of monks.

The Jain tradition is firm on the point that the Principal Scripture consisted of Twelve *aṅgas*. It is generally referred to as the *Dvādaśāṅga-Śruta* in literature. This is also tacitly confirmed by Khāravela who calls it *Coyaṭha Aṁgaṁ, i.e.*, 4+ 8 = 12 *Aṅgas*. He also records that the Principal Scripture[2] had been gradually declining in volume since M.E. 165. This is also in accord with the tradition as already discussed above. The object of the Council was apparently to collect and preserve the remaining canon.[3] Such an attempt had already been made a few decades ago by the Buddhists under the patronage of Aśoka in Magadha.

The institution of worship was present among the Jains. Four types of structures appear to have been built for purposes

1. *Indian Archaeology — A Review*, 1958-59, pp. 38-40, and 1961-62, pp. 36-37.
2. *Mukhiya-kala* = *Mukhya-kala* = Principal Utterance, *i.e.*, the Principal Scripture as uttered by the last Tīrthaṅkara Kevalin Mahāvīra. It is also called *Śruta*, *i.e.*, the knowledge as heard from the Tīrthaṅkara Kevalin.
3. Dr. J.P. Jain traces the origin of the Sarasvatī Movement, *i.e.*, the movement for the redaction of the canonical knowledge among the Jains, to this Council convened by Khāravela (*op. cit.*, p. 117).

of worship: *Kāya-Nisīdīyā* or Relic Memorial in the honour of the *Arahaṁtas* (one was excavated by Khāravela himself), *Nisiyā* or *Caitya*-type structure forming part of monastery (one dedicated by Sindhulā), *Thūpa* or *Stūpa* (worshipped by Khāravela in Mathura), and *Saṁniveśa* or temple housing an image of Jina or *Tīrthaṅkara* (where he worshipped while in Magadha in the twelfth year).[1]

The data recorded in the inscription also suggests that image worship was prevalent among the Jains in Kaliṅga in 424 BC when the image of Jina was taken away by the Nanda king, that Jainism was the personal faith of the king of Kaliṅga and his family, whom the Nanda king had defeated, and that the Nanda king was himself a follower of Jainism since otherwise he would not have taken away the image and installed it in a temple in his capital.[2]

Mathura appears to have been a centre of Jainism in those days and there existed the age-old *Stūpa*, as suggested in the note on the text. Here Khāravela performed the *Savagahanaṁ* ceremony, which was preceded by a procession along with the *Kalpa-Vṛkṣa* (Wish-fulfilling Tree) and was followed by gifts to the Brahmins and worship of the *Arahaṁta*. No such ceremony appears to be mentioned in literature. *Sava-gahanaṁ* = Skt. *Sarva-grahaṇam* can mean both 'All acquisition' and 'All eclipse'. The latter appears to fit more appropriately into the context. It

---

1. Two torsos of naked Jain images were recovered from Lohanipur near Bankipur, Patna. These images might have been installed in that shrine. The Mauryan polish on the larger torso seems to refer to its origin in the Maurya period. The smaller torso, though identical in appearance, style and material, does not have the Mauryan polish, and thus may be earlier in date and possibly represent the Jina image brought from Kaliṅga in the pre-Maurya period.

   Jayaswal thought that a silver punch-marked coin found together with the torsos on the same level, was of variety that preceded the Mauryan coinage (*J.B.O.R.S.*, XXII, pp. 130-32). If so, it would indicate that the shrine where these images were installed, was a pre-Mauryan structure.

2. Ref. App. III, pp. 127-28 *infra*.

seems to suggest that for a time, however short, till the ceremony lasted, he voluntarily eclipsed and withdrew from mundane affairs.

The inscription also contains four symbols; one to the left of L 1-2, the second to the left of L 3-5, the third at the end of L 3, and the fourth at the end of L 16-17. The second and third symbols are respectively *Svastika* and *Nandipada* or *Nandyāvarta*.[1] They are counted among the eight auspicious things required at the time of worship among the Jains. As for the first and fourth symbols which are respectively placed at the beginning and the end of the record, they do not appear to be religious symbols and perhaps represent the royal style of beginning and closing a record by appropriate sealings. Taken in that light the first symbol is probably a replica of crown and the fourth, that of royal standard.

The custom of excavating caves for the use of monks was also prevalent among the Jains, as is evident from the inscriptions in the nearby caves.

---

2. *Svastika* and *Nandyāvarta* have been found portrayed on many Jain Āyāgapaṭṭas of about the beginning of the Christian era, found from Mathura and other sites. See Shah, U.P., *Studies in Jaina Art*, pp. 109-12.

6

Epilogue

BEFORE we conclude, it may be added that Khāravela has not mentioned the Mauryas simply because there was no occasion for it and no inferences can be drawn from this omission. He has mentioned the others only in a context where it was found absolutely necessary to do so since his purpose was not to give a detailed chronological history of Kaliṅga or even of his own dynasty.

The language of the record is Prakrit and the script is Brāhmī. When compared with the records of the Sātavāhanas and other contemporary records, a very curious fact is revealed that 2200 years ago there was no linguistic or scribal controversy in India. This is also the earliest record written in the *kāvya* style so far discovered.

The variety of information preserved in this record gives it a unique place among the sources of history. Such synchronistic, corroborative and authentic information is yet to be found in an epigraph. The evidence preserved in it may help in clearing quite a few of the historical myths created during the last few decades.

Khāravela is firmly and surely placed on the historical map of India. He was the first historical king from the eastern coast to lead such extensive campaigns, and appears to be a more rightful claimant to the glory that has hitherto been given to Samudragupta who came more than 500 yeas after him, in disregard or ignorance of the data preserved in this record.

SECTION II
THE BHABRU EDICT OF AŚOKA

1

Discovery, Text and Translation

THE Bhabru Edict of Aśoka was a chance discovery of one Captain Burt of the late East India Company. It was found inscribed on a detached boulder on the top of the Bījak Pahār on the back of the town of Bairat on the Delhi-Jaipur road, lying 41 miles north of Jaipur, 25 miles west of Alwar and 8 miles and-a-half east "as the crow flies from Bhabru", in Rajasthan. The edict was so named after a camping station at Bhābru or Bhābrā, lying "6 *kos*" to the west of Bairat on the old route from Delhi to Jaipur.[1] It has since been removed to the library of the Asiatic Society of Bengal at Calcutta.

Since this edict specifically mentions certain passages of the sacred Buddhist literature, the mode of addressing the *Saṁgha* and of showing reverence and faith in the Buddha, the *Dharma* and the *Saṁgha*, used by Aśoka are typically Buddhist, and references to the Buddha and his religion as *Bhagavatā Budhena bhāsite save se subhāsite* and *Sadhaṁme chilaṭhitīke hosatīti* have been traced in the Buddhist *Suttas*,[2] it forms one of the most important documents for the history of the Buddhist Church and canonical literature, as also for the personal history of Aśoka, and therefore it has engaged much attention of the Indologists. It was discovered in AD 1840, and the same year Capt. Kittoe and Pt. Kamalā Kānta attempted to decipher it in the *Journal of the Asiatic Society of Bengal*, IX. A systematic

1. Woolner, A.C., *Asoka — Text and Glossary*, Pt. I, Intro. p. xiv.
2. Mookerji, R.K., *Asoka* (2nd rev. edn., 1955), p. 117 fn. 1. The expressions have been traced in the *Aṅguttara* and the *Mahāvyutpatti*.

study of this edict began early in the nineties of the nineteenth century and over a dozen scholars have since laboured on it.

This edict is one of the most well-preserved epigraphs and is contained in eight lines as follows[1]:

L1 Piyadasi[i] Lājā Māgadhe[ii] Saṁghaṁ abhivādanaṁ[iii] āhā apābādhataṁ ca phāsu vihālataṁ cā.

L2 Vidite ve bhaṁte āvatake hamā Budhasi Dhaṁmasi Saṁghasīti galave[iv] caṁ pasāde[v] ca. E keṁchi bhaṁte

L3 Bhagavatā Budhena bhāsite save[vi] se subhāsite vā e cu kho bhaṁte hamiyāye diseyā[vii] hevaṁ Sadhaṁme

L4 cilaṭhitīke hosatīti alahāṁ hakaṁ taṁ vatave[viii]. Imāṁ bhaṁte dhaṁmapaliyāyāni Vinayasamukase

L5 Aliyavasāni Anāgatabhayāni Munigāthā Moneyasūte Upatisapasine e ce Lāghulo-

L6 vāde musāvādaṁ adhigicya Bhagavatā Budhena bhāsite. Etāṁ bhaṁte dhaṁmapaliyāyāni ichāmi

L7 kiṁti bahuke bhikhupāye cā bhikhuniye cā abhikhinaṁ sunayu[ix] cā upadhāleyeyu ca

L8 hevamevā upāsakā cā upāsikā cā. Eteṁ bhaṁte imaṁ likhāpayāmi abhihetaṁ ma jānaṁta ti[x].

---

1. For text, ref. Woolner, *op.cit.*, p. 32; Hultzsch, E., *Corpus Inscriptionum Indicarum*, I, p. 172ff.; Mookerji, *op.cit.*, pp. 212-13; Sircar, D.C., *Select Inscriptions*, I, p. 77; E. Senart, *I.A.*, XX, p. 165ff; B.M. Barua, *I.H.Q.*, II, p. 88.

Alternate readings

Senart — *ii*. Māgadhaṁ

Hultzsch — *i*. Priyadasi *ii*. Māgadhe *iii*. abhivādetūnaṁ *iv*. gālave *v*. prasāde *vi*. sarve *viii*. vātave *ix*. suneyu *x*. abhipretaṁ me jānaṁtū ti.

Barua — *vii*. diseyo *viii*. vitave

This may be rendered into English in the following way:

"Priyadarśi, the King of Magadha, saluting the Saṁgha, and wishing them all health and happiness, thus speaks:

Known is to you, Reverend Sirs, to what extent is my reverence and faith in the Buddha, the Dharma and the Saṁgha.

Whatsoever has been said, Reverend Sirs, by the Lord Buddha, all that has, of course, been well said. But of such, Reverend Sirs, what occurs to me (to be the best) I state that so that the Saddharma (*i.e.*, the religion preached by the Buddha) may be everlasting.

Reverend Sirs, these passages of the scripture as told by the Lord Buddha are the Vinayasamukase (the Buddha's teaching *par excellence*, *i.e.*, the *Dhammacakkapavattana Sutta*), the Aliyavasāni (the *Ariyavaṁsa Sutta*), the Anāgatabhayāni (the *Anāgatabhayāni Sutta*), the Munigāthā (the *Muni Sutta*), the Moneyasūte (the *Nālaka Sutta*), the Upatisapasine (the *Sāriputta Sutta*), and the Lāghulovade (the *Rāhulovada Sutta*) on falsehood.

These passages of the scripture, Reverend Sirs, I desire that most of the monks and nuns should repeatedly listen to and meditate upon, and in the same way the lay disciples, male as well female, (should act).

For this reason, Reverend Sirs, am I causing this to be inscribed that they may know of my intention."[1]

---

1. Dr. B.M. Barua and Dr. Radha Kumud Mookerji (*op. cit.*, pp. 116-18) translated it as follows:

   "His Gracious Majesty, King of Magadha, saluting the Saṁgha and wishing them all health and happiness, addresses them as follows:

   Known is to you, Reverend Sirs, to what extent is my reverence as well as faith in the Buddha, the Dharma and the Saṁgha.

   Whatsoever has been said, Reverend Sirs, by the Lord Buddha, all that has of course been well said. But of such, what has been selected by me that the true Dharma may be everlasting I may be privileged to state.

→

Bhagavatā Budhena bhāsite occurring after *adhigicya* in L 6 should not be taken to qualify only the *Lāghulovāde musāvādaṁ adhigicya*. It appears to qualify *dhaṁmapaliyāyāni* in L 4 since all the texts cited are from the sayings of the Buddha as already stated in lines 2-4 of the edict. It would, therefore, be more appropriate to read *Bhagavatā Budhena bhāsite* with *imāṁ bhaṁte dhaṁmapaliyāyāni* and translate the passage as "Reverend Sirs, these passages of the scripture as told by the Lord Buddha are".

→ The following, Reverend Sirs, are the passages of the scripture:

1. The excellent treatise on Moral Discipline.
2. The course of conduct followed by the Sages — modes of ideal life.
3. Fear of what may come about in future (Danger threatening the Saṁgha and the doctrine).
4. Poem on "who is an hermit?"
5. Discourse on Quietism.
6. The questions of Upatiśya.
7. The sermon to Rāhula beginning with the sermon on falsehood, as delivered by the Lord Buddha.

These sections of the Dharma, Reverend Sirs, I desire that most of the reverend monks and nuns should repeatedly listen to and meditate, and in the same way, the lay disciples, male as well as female, (should act).

For this reason, Reverend Sirs, am I causing this to be inscribed that they may know of my intention."

2

Māgadhe or Māgadhaṁ

THE variants in reading do not make any difference in meaning except in the case of *Māgadhe* or *Māgadhaṁ* in L 1. Hultzsch read *Māgadhe* and treated it to be qualifying *Priyadasi lājā.*[1] According to him, the whole expression would be translated as "Priyadarśi, the king of Magadha". Senart read *Māgadhaṁ* and thought that it qualified *Saṁghaṁ.*[2]

The reading *Māgadhaṁ Saṁghaṁ*, to mean 'the Saṁgha of Magadha', has been generally rejected as the findspot of this edict in far off Rajasthan outside Magadha which traditionally comprised the Patna, Nalanda, Gaya, Rohtas and Bojpur districts of modern Bihar Pradesh, does not bear out the possibility of addressing the Saṁgha as the 'Saṁgha of Magadha'.[3] Since the edict is inscribed on a detached boulder which can be easily transported, it is, however, not quite improbable that it might have been originally placed in a monastery in Magadha and later transplanted in its present findspot in Rajasthan, probably by a mere accident, as there is no evidence to show that a Buddhist monastery existed in the neighbourhood of Bairat in the Mauryan times or immediately afterwards. The presence of Aśoka's Minor Rock Edict I in its neighbourhood does not conclusively associate the place with Buddhism as the other places where recensions of M.R.E. I have been found are not generally sought to be identifed with any

1. Hultzsch, *ibid.*
2. Senart, *ibid.*
3. Mookerji, *op. cit.*, p. 116 fn. 5.

centres of Buddhism.[1] The presence of M.R.E. there simply denotes that Bairat (the ancient Virāṭanagara) was an important place in those days. Its historicity is also borne out from its references in the *Mahābhārata*. The three Schism Edicts, also known as the Minor Pillar Edicts, were rightly set up at Kauśāmbī, Sarnath and Sanchi, which are reputed to be great centres of Buddhism from very early times. The Bhabru Edict should also have been originally instituted at a place which was a great centre of Buddhism and the right place for its setting up would have been the monastery itself as it is addressed directly to the Saṁgha. The isolated evidence of the finding of this edict at the present site is, however, not quite sufficient to make this site a centre of Buddhism in the absence of any other evidence.

But in the absence of any definite proof the theory of transplantation recedes into the realm of mere probabilities. More convincing appears the suggestion of Dr. J.P. Jain that till the promulgation of this edict the Buddhist Saṁgha was still known as the 'Māgadha Saṁgha'. This suggestion of Dr. Jain finds corroboration in Dr. Bhandarkar's view that the Buddhist Saṁgha was undivided till the time of Aśoka.[2] It further leads to the suggestion that by the time of Aśoka the Buddhist Saṁgha was small and was more of local importance and that the real credit for transforming a local sect into a world religion is due to Aśoka, as is also acknowledged by the Buddhists themselves. The inexplicability of Aśoka's styling himself as the 'King of Magadha' in this particularly isolated instance, also tends to support this view. This discussion would make a strong presumption in favour of *Māgadhaṁ Saṁghaṁ*.

---

1. Other findspots are Ahraura, Sasaram, Rupnath, Gujarra, Maski, Gavimadh, Palkigundu, Siddapur, Brahmagiri, Jating-Rameshwar, Yerragudi, Rajula-Mandagiri and Delhi. Ahraura appears to be the only place connected with Buddhism, the findspot being the probable site of the Bhesakalāvana where the Buddha spent one rainy season during his visit to the country of the Bhaggas.
2. Bhandarkar, D.R., *Asoka* (3rd edn., 1955), p. 87.

On the other hand, those favouring *Piyadasi lājā Māgadhe*, seek corroboration in this edict of the Buddhist tradition about the holding of the Buddhist Council (*Saṁgīti*) under Aśoka. Bhandarkar thought that Aśoka should have felt the necessity of introducing himself as 'King of Magadha' as the Council might have been attended by many a Bhikkhu who did not belong to his empire.[1] But this is a mere conjecture[2] in the absence of any reference to the Council in the edict itself. Aśoka has mentioned several events in his edicts and there is no reason to believe that he would not have mentioned such an important event as the convening of the Council, had the edict been promulgated on that occasion. Moreover, the Council met at Pāṭaliputra while the edict has been found hundreds of kilometres away at Bairat.

The extensive distribution of the Aśokan edicts in the different parts of the country also leaves little scope for an inference that the findspot of the edict was outside the empire of Aśoka and hence he introduced himself as 'King of Magadha'. The extreme points are Shar-i-kuna near Kandahar in Afghanistan, Shahbazgarhi and Mansehra near Peshawar and Taxila near Rawalpindi in Pakistan, Kalsi near Dehra Dun in Uttar Pradesh, Rummindei in Nepal, Yerragudi in the Kurnool district in Andhra Pradesh, and Siddapur, Brahmagiri and Jating-Rameshwar in the Chitradurga district in Karnataka Pradesh.

It can be explained better with reference to the administrative divisions under Aśoka. The empire under Aśoka appears to have been divided into five provinces: Magadha directly ruled by the Emperor with headquarters at Pāṭaliputra, and the other provinces of Uttarāpatha with headquarters at Takṣaśilā, Avantiratha with headquarters at Ujjayinī, Dakṣiṇāpatha with headquarters at Suvarṇagiri, and Kaliṅga with headquarters at Tosali, ruled by him through Kumāras or Āryaputras, *i.e.*, the princes of blood royal, acting as his Viceroys.

---

1. Bhandarkar, *op. cit.*, p. 90.
2. V.A. Smith also thinks that it is not addressed to the Council. (*Asoka*, p. 142 fn. 2).

The Magadha province seems to have comprised the erstwhile *janapadas* of Aṅga, Magadha, Kāśī, Kośala, Vajji, Malla, Vatsa, Cedi, Kuru, Pañcāla, Śūrasena and Matsya, its grid being roughly demarcated by the findspots of the Pillar Edicts of Aśoka.[1] Bairat, the traditional capital of Matsya Janapada, fell within the Magadha Province, and since this province was under the direct rule of Aśoka, it was not unnatural for him to style himself as 'King of Magadha' or *Magadha-rāja* in an edict promulgated in that province.

It is also significant that nearer home, in the Barabar Cave Inscriptions, he styles himself as *Piyadasi lājā* and not as *Devānaṁpiya Piyadasi lājā*. *Devānaṁpiya* has been used as a synonym of *rājā* in the different versions of R.E. VIII and K.R.E. II and has also been used as an honorific by his son Daśaratha in his inscriptions. It means that though literally it carries the sense 'beloved of the gods', it was a royal honorific equivalent to 'His Majesty', probably made current during the reign of Aśoka. *Piyadasi*, meaning 'One whose sight is pleasing', was possibly his personal title, and was generally used with the honorific *Devānaṁpiya*, but in his home province he sometimes styled himself simply as *Piyadasi lājā*. The name *Aśoka* appears twice in his edicts, with the appellation of *Devānaṁpiya* only in the Maski recension of his M.R.E. I and complete with *Devānaṁpiya Piyadasi* in the Gujarra recension of the same edict.[2] This seems to settle that both *Devānaṁpiya* and *Piyadasi* were royal honorifics or titles.

In the light of the above discussion the reading *Ṁāgadhe* and the interpretation 'Priyadarśi, the King of Magadha', would appear to be more justified.

---

1. The recensions of P.E. were found at Lauriya-Araraj, Nandangarh and Rampurva in the Champaran district in Bihar, at Kauśāmbī and Meerut in Uttar Pradesh, and at Topra near Ambala in Haryana. The Schism Edicts or Minor P.E. were found at Kauśāmbī and Sarnath in Uttar Pradesh and at Sanchi in Madhya Pradesh, and the Commemorative Pillar Edicts, at Rummindei and Nigliva in South Nepal.

2. Maski Edict — *Devānaṁpiyasa Asokasa*
   Gujarra Edict — *Devānaṁpiyasa Piyadasino Asokarājasa*

3

Identification of Scripture

Of the passages of the Buddhist scripture, referred to by Aśoka, the Aliyavasāni has been identified with the *Ariyavaṁsa Sutta* contained in the *Aṅguttara Catukkanipāta*.[1] The Buddha tells in this *Sutta* that a recluse should not grumble about cloth, food and resting place but should be contented with whatever cloth and food he gets easily and should enjoy meditation.

The Anāgatabhayāni has been identified with the *Anāgatabhayāni Sutta* contained in the *Aṅguttara Pañcakanipāta*.[2] Here the Buddha exhorts the *bhikkhus* to exert all the time lest old age, disease, famine, rebellion or schism should disturb them by creating unfavourable conditions.

The Munigāthā is the *Munisutta* of the *Suttanipāta*.[3] Here the Buddha defines a hermit as one who is homeless, detached, lonely, contented, fearless, above praise or blame, restrained, above sex, and scrupulous about non-killing of and non-injury to living beings and who lives on begging.

The Moneyasūte is the *Nālaka Sutta* of the *Suttanipāta*.[4] This is mainly a sermon on how a *bhikkhu* should behave. It prescribes a code of conduct for the *bhikkhu*s when they go to

---

1. Dharmanand Kosambi, *I.A.*, 1912, pp. 37-40. Earlier Dr. T.W. Rhys Davids sought to identify it with the *Saṁgāti Sutta* (*J.R.A.S.*, 1898, p. 639 ff; *Dialogues of the Buddha*, p. xiii).
2. Kosambi, *ibid.*
3. Rhys Davids, *ibid.*
4. Kosambi, *ibid.*

the villages and asks them mainly to restrain their tongue.

The Upatisapasine has been identified with the *Sāriputta Sutta* of the *Suttanipāta*.[1] Here again the Buddha prescribes a code of behaviour for the *bhikkhus* and forewarns them of the difficulties of their path.

The Lāghulovāde has been identified with the *Rāhulovāda Sutta*, also known as the Cūla Rāhulovāda or the Ambalaṭhika Rāhulovāda, of the *Majjhima Nikāya* (*Sutta* No. 61).[2] *Musāvādaṁ adhigicya* helps in identification. *Adhigicya* has been equated with Sanskrit *adhikṛtya* and is taken to mean 'beginning with' or 'regarding'. Aśoka has not indicated the subject-matter of any other passage and it is difficult to comprehend the necessity that should have occurred to him for indicating the subject-matter in this case. It may be that in his time there were several *Sutta*s known as Rāhulovāda and, therefore, a distinction had to be made by indicating its subject-matter. The sermon begins with a denunciation of falsehood in every conceivable form. The Buddha exhorts Rāhula not to tell a lie even in joke. Thereafter he emphasises the need for critical examination of all bodily, vocal and mental acts.

The identification of Vinayasamukase has, however, been a matter of controversy. Smith[3] and Senart[4] identified it with the First Sermon of the Buddha, better known as the *Dhammacakkapavattana Sutta*. A.J. Edmunds also was of the same view as he discovered in the *Udāna*, iii, that *sāmukkaṁsikā* was used as an adjective of *dhammadesanā*. Kosambi was also later of the same view as he thought that perhaps *vinaya* could also mean 'instruction' and that the First Sermon could have hardly been ignored by Aśoka.[5]

1. Kosambi, *ibid.*, Rhys Davids sought to identify it with certain passages of the *Vinaya*, I.
2. Senart, *ibid.*
3. Smith, V.A., *Oxford History of India*, p. 109.
4. *J.R.A.S.*, 1931, p. 387.
5. Kosambi, Dharmanand, *Bhagavān Buddha*, (Hindi, 1956), pp. 7-8.

But Barua and other scholars were guided by *Vinaya* in its traditional meaning in their identification of this passage. Barua identified it with the *Sigalovāda Suttanta* of the *Dīgha Nikāya* which, according to the commentary of Buddhaghosa, contains *Gihivinaya* and thus applies to the house-holders as well. The Suttanta further deals with *Ariyasavinaya* or the *Vinayasamukase* in Aśokan parlance which is nothing but the 'Ideal Discipline'. It also thus applies to all classes, to monks and nuns as well as to lay disciples, for whose study Aśoka intended it.[1] S.N. Mitra, however, identified it with the *Sappurisa Sutta* of the *Majjhima Nikāya* as the words *vinayadhara* and '*attāna ukkaṁseti*' (= *sāmukaso*) occur in that passage.[2] C.D. Chatterji traced the clue to the identification of the various passages mentioned by Aśoka in a story narrated by Buddhaghosa in the *Visuddhimagga*. It depicts an ideal monk who followed the code of conduct prescribed by the Buddha in the *Rathavinīta Sutta*, the *Nālaka Sutta*, the *Mahā Ariyavaṁsa* and the *Tuvaṭaka Sutta*, the first three, according to Chatterji, being the same as the Upatisapasine, the Moneyasūte and the Aliyavasāni of Aśoka. He equates the *Tuvaṭaka Sutta* in which the Buddha discourses on *pāṭipāda, pātimokkha*, and *samādhi*, with the Vinayasamukase of Aśoka as these discourses may well make up the cream of *Vinaya*, and he feels, what Buddhaghosa selected as the most important and representative for a *bhikkhu* might well have been cited by Aśoka too.[3]

The edict is, in fact, meant for the monks and nuns as well as the lay disciples. The other passages besides laying down the code for clergy, are also meant for the laity. The main object of Aśoka in asking the laity to read and meditate upon these passages appears to be simply to enjoin on the laity the duty to see that the clergy did not degenerate. This duty could be

---

1. *J.R.A.S.*, 1915, p. 809.
2. *I.A.*,1919, pp. 8-11.
3. Mookerji, *op. cit.*, pp. 117-18 fn. 8. D.C. Sircar identified the first text with the Atthavasavagga contained in the *Aṅguttara* (*J.D.L.*, XX).

discharged efficiently only if the laity knew the standards by which to judge a monk or nun.

It would thus be wrong to surmise that Aśoka was laying down the rules of conduct for monks and nuns alone. It also passes comprehension that Aśoka should have ignored the first sermon which forms the very basis of the entire Buddhist philosophy, the *sāra* of the Buddha's teachings in Aśokan parlance. The first sermon really deserved the first place and was rightly mentioned first by Aśoka as Vinayasamukase.

Root *ni* with prefix *vi* has been used in the meaning of 'to instruct, to educate, to direct' in the *Mahābhārata*, and the word *vinaya* itself has been used to mean 'education, discipline, control, leading, guidance, training (moral)' in the same Epic.[1] In the Pāli canon also *ni* with prefix *vi* has been used in the meaning of 'to teach'.[2]

Although in the Pāli canon *samukkaṁsa* does not appear in the meaning of 'teachings of the Buddha', the expression *sāmukkaṁsika* occurs at several places as comprising the Four Noble Truths, namely, *Dukkhaṁ*, *Samudayaṁ*, *Nirodhaṁ* and *Maggaṁ*, expounded in the First Sermon.[3]

In the light of the above discussion it would be only logical to interpret Vinayasamukase (Skt. *Vinaya-samut-karśaḥ* =the Vinaya *par excellence*) as the Buddha's teaching *par excellence* and identify it with the First Sermon or the *Dhammacakka-pavattana* Sutta. It is just possible that in the days of Aśoka that sermon was actually known as named by him.

---

1. Monier-Willams, M., *A Sanskrit-English Dictionary*, p. 971.
2. For example, *Aṅguttara*, IV, Sutta 111, and *Majjhima*, Suttas 107 and 147, cited by Kosambi, *op. cit.*, p. 7.
3. Ref. the Upāli Sutta in the *Majjhima Nikāya* and the Ambaṭṭha Sutta in the *Dīgha Nikāya*. The concluding portion of the Ambaṭṭha Sutta:

   Yadā bhagavā aññāsi brahmaṇaṁ Pokkharasatiṁ kallacittaṁ muducittaṁ vinivaraṇacittaṁ udaggacittaṁ pasantacittaṁ atha yā Buddhānaṁ sāmukkaṁsikā dhammadesanā taṁ pakāsesi dukkhaṁ samudayaṁ nirodhaṁ maggaṁ.

4

Buddhism and Aśoka

SENART has pointed out that it is strange that if the Buddhist canon was defined and closed by the time of Aśoka, as stated in the southern legends, he should select for indicating the Buddha's lessons pieces so little characteristic, so short and so devoid of dogmatic importance as those which he cites appear to be, and that, too, without even alluding to the great collection of which the title alone would have been infinitely more significant and to which it would be so natural to appeal when addressing the Saṁgha.[1] Several of the Buddhist scholars have also since expressed doubts about the correctness of the southern legends.[2] Three of the seven passages mentioned by Aśoka have been traced in the *Suttanipāta* of the *Khuddaka Nikāya* of the *Suttapiṭaka*. They are in verse. Of the remaining passages, two have been traced in the *Aṅguttara Nikāya* and one in the *Majjhima Nikāya* of the same *piṭaka*. It is difficult to draw any inference from this but it may be said that the *Suttanipāta* perhaps represents the oldest collection of the Buddha's teachings and perhaps also the verse portions are older than others. It is just possible that the *Vinayapiṭaka* as it is known today, did not exist then and perhaps only a very contracted version of the *Suttapiṭaka* represented the teachings of the Buddha.

The Southern legends only hint towards an attempt at consolidating the teachings of the Buddha in the time of Aśoka.

---

1. Senart, E., *Les Inscriptiones de Piyadasi*.

2. Kosambi, *op. cit.*, pp. 6-7.

It would be wrong to assume that the whole canon was defined and closed then. It was, in fact, in a process of evolution and this process continued at least till the first century of the Christian Era. Additions and alterations must have been continuously made suiting to the exigencis of time and land. This tendency is more clearly exhibited in the development of the various schools.

The evidence afforded within the inscriptions of Aśoka suggests that he did not cause any edict to be incised on rocks and pillars earlier than his twelfth regnal year. The earliest of his records are R.E. I-IV, M.R.E. I-II, and the two Barabar Cave Inscriptions, of the Year 12. In M.R.E. I he declares his association with the Saṁgha for the first time. He refers to his visit to the Saṁgha and to the installation of the Buddha's relics, as also to his setting out on pilgrimage, in this edict. His visit to the Saṁgha referred to therein could not have been the occasion for giving instructions to the Saṁgha. The position of the Schism Edict on the Allahabad Pillar just below P.E. I-VI suggests that the Schism Edicts were issued in the Year 26 simultaneously with P.E. I-VI. Aśoka assumes the role of the mentor of the Saṁgha in the Schism Edicts. He also ordains the laity to be mindful of the conduct of the monks and nuns so that they may not violate his orders. This was also the occasion when he should have thought it fit to prescribe compulsory study of certain passages of the scripture so that all members of the congregation might be reminded of the fundamentals of the Buddha's teachings as well as of the ideal conduct prescribed for the *bhikṣus* and *bhikṣuṇīs*. The Bhabru Edict thus appears to have been issued at the same time as the Schism Edicts. Possibly there were more recensions of this edict, supplied to all the important monastic establishments, but unfortunately only one recension is now available. It is not addressed to a particularly local Saṁgha but it is addressed to the Saṁgha generally. By its very nature it appears to be supplementing the Schism Edicts and seems to confirm the assumption of mentor's role by Aśoka *vis-a-vis* the Saṁgha in his later days.

The schismatic tendencies in the Buddhist Saṁgha had made their ugly appearance during the life-time of the Buddha himself. After Aśoka had extended royal patronage to Buddhism, made a serious attempt to consolidate the Buddha's teachings by convening a Buddhist Council and planned systematic programme for propagating them not only within his empire but also in foreign lands by sending missionaries, it was only natural for him to deal with such tendencies with a firm hand. The action appears to have been two-fold: educative as in the Bhabru Edict and punitive as in the Schism Edicts.

Aśoka has spoken of his diligence in several edicts. The Bhabru Edict is an example of his diligence; it not only settles the controversy about his conversion to Buddhism but it also portrays him as a diligent Buddhist who had studied the scripture and obtained such mastery of the religious tenets that he could recommend even to the Saṁgha what it should specially read.

He was, however, not a bigot. Buddhism was his personal faith and although he did much for its propagation, he was tolerant of the different creeds and gave patronage to all alike as a king. This tradition of secularism was followed by all the great kings of ancient India. Khāravela, coming fifty years after Aśoka, was a follower of Jainism and his services to Jainism were also comparable to those of Aśoka to Buddhism, but he took pride in styling himself as 'the embellisher of all temples' and as 'the worshipper of all religions'.

SECTION III

PRAKRIT AND BRĀHMĪ

1

Genesis of the Prakrit Languages

NAMISĀDHU seems to have struck the right note when he explains the word *prākṛta* as derived from *prakṛti* in the sense of natural speech free from the rules of grammarians.[1] He wrote it in AD 1068 when the literary forms of Prakrit had already been fossilised. The other explanation offered by him, deriving it from *prāk kṛta*, to mean 'created of old',[2] is in consonance with his faith that the language of the *Ārṣa* canon, Ardha-Māgadhī, is the language of the gods,[3] and is not very relevant to a philological discussion.

In the sixties of the nineteenth century E.B. Cowell brought out Vararuci's *Prākṛta-Prakāśa* with the Manoramā commentary of Bhāmaha, and thenceforth Prakrit has engaged the attention of many linguists and Indologists. The pioneers in the field are Hermann Jacobi, Richard Pischel, A.F.R. Hoernle, George Bühler, Sten Konow, A.C. Woolner, Muni Jina Vijaya, Banarasi Das Jain and A.N. Upadhye. The linguistic survey of George Grierson, the philological deliberations of Suniti Kumar Chatterji, the volumes of Maurice Winternitz on the history of Indian literature, the discovery of Prakrit and Sanskrit texts, and an in-depth study of the Pāli, Prakrit, Apabhraṁśa and Sanskrit works, as also of the epigraphic and numismatic material, during the last one-hundred-thirty years or so, have

---

1. *Vide* Namisādhu's commentary on Rudraṭa's *Kāvyālaṁkāra*, 2, 12.
2. *Ibid.*
3. *Ārisa-vayaṇe siddhaṁ devāṇaṁ Addhamāgahā vāṇī.*

expanded and elaborated the problem of the linguistic bases of the Indian panorama.

During all this effort a bias was assiduously tilted towards finding some remote ancestry to link the Indian intelligentsia with the Eruo-Anglican rulers, to build up the myth that India was a no-man's land and it was filled by the *Dāsa* (Dravidians), *Niṣāda* (Austrics), *Kirāta* (Mongoloids) and *Ārya* (Nordics, the vast Indo-European community, branching off to the Indo-Iranian from which shot out the Indo-Aryans who composed the Vedas in the *Sapta-Sindhu*), and lastly, to consign the entire literary effort, nay the speech effort itself, to the Indo-Aryan genius as if whoever preceded them were a mute people. The fallacy of this stupendous task is obvious but the emotional strains ingrained therein dissuade from an objective appraisal.

To put it briefly, the Indian linguistic history has been built up on the premise that there are three strata of language development in India, firstly the Old Indo-Aryan representing successively the Vedic, the Brāhmaṇa and the classical Sanskrit (developed out of the Udīcya or northern dialect of the Vedic Aryans and codified by Pāṇini); secondly, the Middle Indo-Aryan, representing the Prakrits developing out of the Madhyadeśīya and Prācya dialects of the Vedic Aryans, and the Apabhraṁśa, a further debasement of the *Devabhāṣā*; and lastly, the New Indo-Aryan representing different *vibhāṣā* which finally emerged as the present-day vernaculars.

Three potent factors have been kept out of sight in projecting this development. One such factor is that Sanskrit was confined to a small minority which assiduously maintained its aloofness from the masses; the masses spoke different tongues which were the so many patois hardly related to Sanskrit. The second important factor is that there is specific evidence on record that a *lingua franca* was in vogue throughout the sub-continent as far north-west as the Kabul valley, as far north as the Nepalese Tarai, as far east as the Bengal coast, as far south as the North Penner and as far west as Saurāṣṭra, which was intelligible to and used by the people in general with slight phonetic variations, and was written and read in a common script throughout the land to the south and east of the Sutlej, much in the same way as Hindi written in Devanagari is intelligible to all Indians today except when they take a stance like the Sanskrit-*niṣṭha* Brahmins of Aśoka Maurya's days, *e.g.*, the Urdu protagonists, or get worked up with regional chauvinism fanned for political ends. And the third substantial factor is that out of the numerous dialects only one becomes the *koine* or literary norm, just as *Khaḍī-bolī* is the koine of Hindi language and Meridian dialect is the koine of English language and that grammar follows, and does not precede, the language. The people's language is represented by the Aśokan edicts and the numerous records of the Sātavāhanas, Śuṅgas and Kaliṅgas, as also of the Greeks, Śakas and Kuṣāṇas, up to the second century AD. What has come down to us as the Prakrit literature, be it Pāli of the Buddhists, Mahārāṣṭrī and Śaurasenī as well as Ardha-Māgadhī of the Jains, or Māgadhī, Mahārāṣṭrī, Śaurasenī and Paiśācī Prakrit of the Sanskrit dramatists, at the time of its redaction the literary form had already been fossilised and, if not never, it seldom represented the popular medium. Although Vararuci, who wrote Vārttikas on Pāṇini and lived probably in fifth century AD, is the first to give a grammar for Prakrit, and Bhāmaha (assigned to the seventh century AD) wrote commentary on it, the most important of the Prakrit grammars is the chapter VIII of the *Siddha-Hemacandra* of Hemacandra Sūri (AD 1088-1172) and interestingly all these grammarians were Sanskritists who added only a chapter on Prakrit in their work on Sanskrit grammar. This can explain that the literary Prakrit as extant now was systematised, and the works were possibly cleansed of colloqualisms by the learned puṇḍits to bring them in tune with the grammatical codes and at par with the language of the *śiṣṭa* (urbanised, in essence, an adept in the use of chaste Sanskrit) of the day.

The language used by Aśoka Maurya (272-236 BC) in his inscriptions provides us with a window on the language of the masses in the first millennium before Christ. According to the phonetic variations, four groups are indicated:

1. The region to the west of the Sutlej, falling within the Viceroyalty of Takṣaśilā, and represented by the Rock Edicts at Shahbazgarhi and Mansehra. Besides the Indian language written in the Kharoṣṭhi script, the Greek and Aramaic languages written in their respective scripts were also in use, mostly beyond the Khyber and Bolan passes.
2. The region to the east and south of the Sutlej, covering the entire Gangetic basin, with centre at Pāṭaliputra, and represented by the Rock Edicts at Kalsi, Dhauli and Jaugad, Pillar Edicts in Haryana, Uttar Pradesh and Bihar, and the Minor Rock and Pillar Edicts in Rajasthan, Uttar Pradesh, Madhya Pradesh and Bihar — all written in Prakrit but in the Brāhmī script.
3. The region controlled by the Viceroyalty of Ujjayinī, and represented by the Rock Edicts at Girnar and Sopara, written in Prakrit in the Brāhmī script.
4. The region controlled by the Viceroyalty at Suvarṇagiri, and represented by the Edicts in Andhra Pradesh and Karnataka Pradesh, written in Prakrit in the Brāhmī script.

The same form of language and script continued for about 500 years after Aśoka when it was supplanted by panegyrics and eulogies in classical Sanskrit of the *kāvya* style. The earliest of the inscriptions in Sanskrit is the Sudarśana Lake Inscription of Rudradāman dated in AD 150 and the most important of the lucid panegyrics (*praśasti*) is that of Hariṣeṇa composed for Samudragupta and inscribed on the Aśokan pillar at Allahabad in *c*. AD 360. Incidentally, both the above records are preserved on the same sites which contain Aśoka's records. Earlier to Rudradāman's records, there are only three pieces in Sanskrit: one is a small inscription of one Dhana claiming to be sixth in descent from Puṣyamitra who had performed two Horse-sacrifices, and is from Ayodhya; the other two are known as the Ghoshundi and Hathiwara grants and their provenance is near Jaipur; they cannot be pushed beyond the beginning of the Christian Era. It is curious to note that despite the projected zeal of the Śuṅgas for the revival of Brahmanical ritualism and reinstatement of Sanskrit scholarship, all the Śuṅga records known so far are in Prakrit, and a Greek, Heliodorus by name, who consecrated a *Garuḍa-dhvaja* to propitiate Viṣṇu in the kingdom of Śuṅga Bhāgbhadra at Vidisha, possibly the capital, also made his record in Prakrit in the Brāhmī script. The best narrative record from the historical point of view is that of Khāravela who got it recorded in *c.* 172 BC on the Hāthigumphā on the Udayagiri near Bhubaneshwar in Orissa, in Prakrit in the Brāhmī script, continuing the tradition of the Mauryan administration. This tradition was also continued by the Sātavāhanas in the Narmada-Godavari valley, whence they carried it down to Kanchipuram where they created the *Thoṇḍimaṇḍalam* and founded the Pallava Kingdom with Prakrit as the court language.[1] The dynasty of Khāravela as well as that of the Sātavāhanas or Āndhra-bhṛtyas, were founded by the servants, possibly of the Mahāmātra rank, of the Maurya Empire.

Just as inscriptions in Sanskrit were rare before AD 150 so were inscriptions in Prakrit rare after the Gupta period, say AD 500 onwards. A notable example is provided by the record of Kakkuka, found near Ghatayala in Jodhpur District, dated in Saṁvat 918 (AD 861). It is in *kāvya* style, composed in chaste Jain Mahārāṣṭrī, and contains 23 verses, recording the founding of a Jain temple, establishing of a market and erecting of two pillars, and *inter alia* mentions the curious fact that he had descended from a Brahmin father and a Kṣatriya mother.[2]

---

1. Ref. A. Chakravartinayanar's Historical Introduction to *Pañcāstikāyasāra*, pp. ix-xii.
2. *J.R.A.S.*, 1855, Vol: 27, p. 513; Woolner, A.C., *Introduction to Prakrit*, pp. 146-51.

The Jains and the Buddhists maintain that Mahāvīra and the Buddha had preached in the people's language. Among the Jains, the Śvetāmbara Āgamas are in Ardha-Māgadhī and the early Digambara works in Jain Śauraseni. The Theravāda Buddhist canon is in Pāli. The area of both Mahāvīra and the Buddha was the same, namely, eastern Uttar Pradesh and north and central Bihar. Therefore the language of the two teachers ought to be the same because they wandered among the same people. But then why this divergence is there, has been a baffling question.

A key to this riddle is provided by the language of the Aśokan edicts, especially his Calcutta-Bairat inscription where he quotes certain passages from the scripture. It postulates that there must have been some collection from which he drew upon and it was possibly in the Māgadhī as spoken in that region (Region No. 2 above). The discovery of Aśvaghoṣa's plays in Khotan further indicated that they were in a Prakrit not akin to Pāli,[1] and hence it would not be pertinent to suppose that the Buddha spoke Pāli. Woolner notes, "Pāli originally meaning a 'boundary, limit, or line' was applied to the *canon* of the Hīnayāna Buddhists. Thence it is used of the *language* of that *canon*, found also in some canonical books: all being preserved in what were originally the missionary churches of Ceylon, Burma and Siam."[2] He also notes that Pāli is not Māgadhī. It has been supposed that it might be the language of Ujjain whence Mahendra took the sacred Canon to Ceylon, or it might be the language of the Kaliṅga country because of certain resemblances with the language of Khāravela's record, or it might be from some place near the Vindhyas because of some points of resemblance with Paiśācī, or it might be an old form of Śaurasenī. Woolner concludes, "Whatever may be the exact truth of the matter, it is clear that Pāli contains several different strands in its composition and that it varies also according to its age. The

1. Woolner, *op. cit.*, p. 74; Lüders, *Bruchstucke Buddhstischer Dramen.*
2. Woolner, *op. cit.*, p. 71.

oldest type is seen in the *Gāthās*, then come the prose portions of the Canon followed by non-canonical literature and finally still later layers. The development of Pāli has been influenced by Sanskrit."[1]

Similarly as the Brahmins detested the *Vrātyas* who did not owe allegiance to the Vedic fire-cult and the Brahmanic social and religous organisation and called the *Prācyas* or Easterners as being *āsurīya* or demoniac, *i.e.*, barbarian and hostile in nature,[2] so the *Prācya Vrātya* thinkers boycotted Sanskrit and discarded the Brahmanic concept of social discrimination. The Buddha accordingly bade his followers to learn his teachings in their own language,[3] and thus the ground was prepared where the original teachings could be redacted in different dialects.

The Theravāda Canon was reduced to writing in the first century BC. Winternitz aptly notes that 'the monks of Ceylon were bent on preserving and passing on the texts written in the language once established for them in India. In all probability these monks were just as conscientious regarding the contents as regarding the language, and preserved and handed down to us the texts of the *Tipiṭaka* which was written down in the Pāli language, with rare fidelity during the last two thousand years."[4]

---

1. Woolner, *op.cit.*, pp. 72-73.
2. Chatterji, S.K., *Indo-Aryan and Hindi*, pp. 60-61.
3. *Ibid.*, p. 64. When two Brahmin disciples of the Buddha suggested that his teachings should be translated into the learned man's tongue (Sanskrit) from the very debased vernacular of the East (*Prācya* dialect), he refused to accept the suggestion and, instead, recommended that men should study his word 'each in his own language' (*sakāya niruttiyā*). (*vide*, *Culla-vagga*, v 33; *cf. Majjhima-Nikāya* 139). Also refer Winternitz, W., *A History of Indian Literature*, Vol. II, pp. 601-05.
4. Winterntz, *op. cit.*, p. 14.

The redaction of the Jain Canon followed a more devious route. There is a tradition that there was a twelve-year famine in Magadha about 150 years after the *nirvāṇa* of Mahāvīra when a portion of the Saṁgha migrated to South India under the leadership of Bhadrabāhu I, the last of the *Śruta-kevalin*s. After the famine a Council was convened by the members of the Saṁgha who had stayed behind in the north, for the restoration of the sacred canon, as so many monks who were the repositories of the sacred lore, had been dead. The representatives from the south did not join it, nor they accepted the Canon so compiled by the ascetics of the north who had become slack in ascetic practices to some extent due to the exigencies of famine. Thus followed the Schism as the Digambaras and the Śvetāmbaras. The Śvetāmbaras finally redacted the Canon as preserved with them at the Pāṭaliputra Council, under Devardhigaṇi at Vallabhī in M.E. 983 (AD 456).[1] In course of time, as it passed through word of mouth it was affected by the regional dialects to some extent, but in essence retained an archaic character in language. This was termed as Ardha-Māgadhī. It appears to be the Māgadhī which was largely influenced by Śaurasenī. The Saṁgha that travelled to South India, redacted their pro-canonical literature in the Prakrit that they had brought with them. A.N. Upadhye calls it *Jain Śaurasenī*.[2] He has traced common verses in the South Indian Digambara pro-canonical literature and the Śvetāmbara Ardha-Māgadhī Āgama literature, and has concluded that it proves their common heritage.[3] The redaction of the Digambara literature started with Kunda-kunda who succeeded to pontificate in 8 BC. He wrote in Prakrit (Jain Śaurasenī) 84 *Pāhuḍas*.[4] The Śvetāmbaras took

1. A.N. Upadhye's Introduction to *Pravacanasāra*, p. 177; Winternitz, *op. cit.*, pp. 431-35.
2. Upadhye, *op. cit.*, pp. 115-17.
3. *Ibid.*, pp. 113-15, 123.
4. Jain, J.P., *The Jaina Sources of the History of Ancient India*, pp. 120-26.

to writing some 450 years after Kunda-kunda. Their centre had shifted from Magadha to Ujjayinī, and later on to Vallabhī, which factor contributed to their taking to Mahārāṣṭrī Prakrit for their pro-canonical literature. Distinct from the literary Prakrit used in Sanskrit dramas, the Mahārāṣṭri Prakrit was the *lingua franca* of the region and was used as vehicle for their compositions by the Śvetāmbara Jains particularly, so it came to be identified as the Jain Mahārāṣṭri. The material point to be noted here is that as the Pāli survived in a form in which it reached Sri Lanka, so the Ardha-Māgadhī, Jain Śaurasenī and Jain Mahārāṣṭri survived in a form in which they were once adopted by the two sects of the Jains, and this survival was possible for two reasons — one was the seclusion and removal from the centre of their origin, and the other was the sanctity imposed on the scripture as *Ārṣa*, hence not subject to interference *prima facie*.

It is inferred from Hāthīgumphā Inscription of Khāravela of Kaliṅga that a Council of monks for the recitation of the Canon was convened 355 years after Mahāvīra's *nirvāṇa*, *i.e.*, in 172 BC. There is no mention of this Council either in the Śvetāmbara or in the Digambara literature. There is a possibility that an attempt was then made to reconcile the Schism, or it might have been simply a congregation of the Digambara monks, but nothing definite can be said.

The foregoing discussion postulates a review of our approach to the study of Prakrit languages and to tracing the linguistic developments in India in an objective manner, taking Prakrit as *prākṛta* and Sanskrit as *saṁskṛta* modes of expression and basing it on the Indian scene first of all.

2

Tradition of Writing, and Scripts, in Ancient India

THE discovery of a script on seals belonging to the chalcolithic civilisation of the Indus Valley, has established the tradition of writing in India as far back as 3500 BC at least and has belied the speculations of the 'import' theory enthusiasts. Its points of resemblance with the Egyptian, the Sumerian and the Proto-Elamite scripts have been analysed by G.R. Hunter:

> The entire body of anthropomorphic signs have Egyptian equivalents which are virtually exact; these signs have no parallels in the Sumerian or the Proto-Elamite.
>
> There are many of the signs that are exactly paralleled in the Proto-Elamite and Jemdet-Nasr tablets; they have no conceivable morphological equivalent in the Egyptian.
>
> There is a considerable proportion of signs that are common to all the three scripts, such as the signs for tree, bird, fish.
>
> The less obvious and more conventionalised ideograms, especially those that are so conventionalised that their pictographic origin is hardly determinable, show a marked correspondence, and in a lesser degree, as in the Proto-Elamite, where easily recognisable pictographs show the same variations.

He concludes that "it is possible that all three had a common ancestry, and that the Egyptian element in our script alone was borrowed. It is even possible that all four scripts may have had a common origin."[1] It is accepted by all savants who have worked on the ancient civilisations in the Nile, Euphrates and Indus valleys, that there was intercommunication. There is not much evidence to support the hypothesis that these civilisations had a common ancestry. In the present state of our knowledge, as borne out by the analysis of Hunter as well, the safe surmise would be that the three civilisations developed independently and the scripts they gave were products of indigenous effort, but in course of time they benefitted and enriched by mutual intercourse. Such instances of mutual communion are known throughout the known course of history to date among the developed peoples.

The Indus Valley script appears to consist of ideographs, morphographs and phonographs. Efforts at its decipherment are eluding because of one basic factor that a narrative inscription has yet to be discovered. The specimens have been found on seals, mainly clay tablets, the specific purpose of which is yet to be determined. They, however, prove the fundamental that the art of writing or redacting thoughts morphologically, was invented in the Indus Valley not later than any other civilised community hitherto known.

The common writing material has always been perishable media. If today, despite all the scientific and technological advancement, we are unable to create paper which would last longer than a few hundred years with all the best care, we should not wonder if manuscripts on *bhurja-patra* (birch-bark) or *tāḍa-patra* (palm-leaf) or some variety of paper or wood are not found

---

1. *The Script of Harappa and Mohenjodaro and its connection with other scripts*, pp. 45-47.

   K.N. Dikshit (*Prehistoric Civilisation of the Indus Valley*, p. 40) and R.B. Pandey (*Indian Palaeography*, pp. 34-35) would have us believe that the Nile and Euphrates civilisations were also the product of the Aryan genius of Indian origin. David Diringer (*The Alphabet*, p. 85) is on the other extreme and finds it hard to believe that script could originate in the Indus Valley.

beyond a millennium. Inscribed copper or silver carries us only as far as the beginning of the Christian Era. The best preserved specimens are on stone, and a few on clay, that take us as far back as the middle of the sixth century BC. But they provide positive evidence that writing was a common-place thing at that time. Moulding in clay and incision in stone could follow only after the draft had been written down on a common medium. Moulders and engravers would be more usually copyists though in some cases they could be calligraphists as well. This discussion leads us to the suggestion that there could not have been a void between the known specimens of the Indus Valley script, at the lower limit dating back to the second millennium BC, and the Piprahwa Vase Inscription which records the dedication of a relic casket of the Buddha by his Śākya brethren presumably immediately after his *parinirvāṇa* in 544 BC.[1] This is also indicated by the mass of literature in the form of Vedic Saṁhitās, Brāhmaṇas and Upaniṣads, and Sramanic philosophies, besides grammar which Pāṇini, in *c.* eighth century BC, stylised and codified quoting earlier authorities. The grammar of Pāṇini presupposes the morphology of *akṣara* or letter; the roots *paṭh* (to read) and *likh* (to write) are positive indications.

The extant specimens of earliest Indian scripts fall into two categories. One set is called the Brāhmī Script which was written from left to right and was in use throughout the vast expanse of the Indian subcontinent to the east of the R. Sutlej. It is possible to trace the development of modern Indian scripts from the Brāhmī from sixth century BC onwards. It was a fully developed script in the sixth century BC, with letters divided into vowels and consonants and with medials and phonetics.

The other set is called the Kharoṣṭi script which was written from right to left. It was in use to the west of the R. Sutlej, mainly around Taxila in the Sindhu-Jhelum Doab and the Swat

1. Sukitibhatinaṁ Sabhaginikanaṁ saputadalanaṁ
Iyaṁ salilanidhane Budhasa bhagavate Sakiyānaṁ
— *I.A.*, XXXVI, p. 17ff.

Piprahwa is in the Siddharthnagar district of Uttar Pradesh.

valley during third ceutury BC to fourth century AD. To the east of the Sutlej it was brought to Mathura on the western bank of the R. Yamuna by the Śaka Satraps who preceded the Kuṣāṇas, in the first century BC. The Śakas, however, did not carry it to Saurāṣṭra and Ujjayinī where they used the Brāhmī in vogue there. It has only short vowels and short medials, and lesser number of letters as compared to the Brāhmī. Its currency in India to the west of the Sutlej also ceased by the fourth century AD and traces of any developmental sequence as in the case of the Brāhmī, are also not available.

The decipherment of the Brāhmī and Kharoṣṭi characters was a long and arduous task. It took nearly a century to complete the job. Contributions of James Prinsep, George Bühler and Alexander Cunningham are significant. Nomenclature was made easy by the *Fa-Wan-Shu-Lin*, the Chinese Encyclopaedia composed in AD 668. It records that the invention of writing was made by three divine powers: the first of these was Fan (Brahmā), who invented the Brāhmī script, which runs from the left to the right; the second divine power was Kia-lu (Kharoṣṭa) who invented Kharoṣṭi, which runs from the right to the left; and the third and the least important was Tsam-ki, the script invented by whom runs from the up to the down. It also informs that the first two divine powers were born in India and the third in China.[1]

The Edicts of Aśoka in both Brāhmī and Kharoṣṭi scripts provide positive evidence that both these scripts were in use in the third century BC. Rare manuscripts of the *Dhammapada* and other Buddhist works have been found in Khotan beyond the Karakoram in Central Asia which show that though the Kharoṣṭi script was forgotten in the land of its birth, it continued to be in use beyond its borders through the missionaries of Buddhism and could claim a place of honour in the Chinese Encyclopaedia in the seventh century AD.

1. *Babylonian and Oriental Records*, I. 59; Pandey, R.B., *Indian Palaeography*, p. 25.

It is a strange fact that the names of these scripts are not found in the Brahmanical literature. Pāṇini also mentions only the *Yavanāni-lipi* as an illustration.[1] Aśoka also ignores to give the name of the scripts used by him when he enumerates so many other things in his Pillar Edict VII. The *Lalitavistara*, biography of the Buddha in Sanskrit, dateable in the second-third century AD which had been translated into the Chinese in AD 308, gives a list of 64 scripts. The list begins with Brāhmī and Kharoṣṭi, and includes such regional scripts as Puṣkarasāri (of Puṣkalāvatī), Aṅga, Vaṅga, Magadha, Draviḍa, Kanāri, Dakṣiṇa, Uparagauḍa and Pūrvavideha, besides tribal scripts such as Śakāri, Darada, Khasya, Nāga, Yakṣa, Gandharva, Kinnara and Garuḍa, and foreign scripts named Cīna, Hūṇa, Asura and Uttarakurudvīpa. The remaining names seem to suggest styles and are not of any help in identifying the scripts. The list does not mention the Yavana or Greek script, possibly because by the time of its composition the Greek script had ceased to be in use in India.

According to the Jain tradition, Ṛṣabhanātha, the first Tīrthaṅkara, had taught his two daughters Brāhmī and Sundarī respectively the alphabets and numerals, and hence the script was called after Brāhmī and came to be known as the Brāhmī. The *Bhagavatīsūtra* makes salutation to the Brāhmī script (*Namo Baṁbhiye liviye*). The *Pannavanāsūtra* and the *Samavāyāṁgasūtra* give a list of 18 scripts. The list begins with Baṁbhī and places Kharoṭṭhi at No. 4. It includes regional scripts such as Dosapuriyā, Pukkharasariyā, Bhogavaigā, Pahārāiya and Dāmili, and tribal scripts named Gaṁdhavva and Poliṁdi. The only foreign script named is Javanāli or Javanāliya (Greek) and it is mentioned at No. 2; this suggests that the list is older than the *Lalitavistara* list; the Greek script was in use in the Seleucid Provinces ceded by Seleukos to Candragupta Maurya, was used by the Indo-Greeks, Indo-Parthians, Indo-Scythians and the Kuṣāṇas in the Upper Indus (now in Pakistan), and Vāsudeva (AD 139-170) of the House of

1. *Aṣṭādhyāyī*, III.2.21.

Kaniṣka was the last ruler to use it on his coins. Names common to the lists of the *Lalitavistara* and the Jain Sūtras are Brāhmī and Kharoṣṭi, the regional Puṣkarasāri and Draviḍa, and the tribal Gandharva.

The first positive evidence of the prevalence of different scripts is provided by the widespread inscriptions of Aśoka. To the east of the R. Sutlej all his inscriptions are only in one script — the Brāhmī, but to the west of the Sutlej his inscriptions have been found in three scripts — the Kharoṣṭi, the Aramaic and the Greek. Inscriptions in the Aramaic script and language have been discovered at Taxila (Rawalpindi district, Pakistan), Pule-Darunt (Laghman, near Jalalabad, Afghanistan) and Shar-i-Kuna (near Kandahar, Afghanistan). The Shar-i-Kuna record is bilingual and it has a recension in the Greek script and language as well. A record only in the Greek script and language has also been found at Kandahar. Two recensions of Aśoka's 14 Rock Edicts have been found incised in the Kharoṣṭi script and Prakrit language at Mansehra (Hazara district) and Shahbazgarhi (near Charsadda, Peshawar district) in North-West Pakistan.

In interpreting the palaeographic evidence two factors should also be kept in view, namely the scribe's hand and the material on which the matter is inscribed. Change in general contours of letters takes a long time to take effect. In that light the stages in the development of Brāhmī script would be Aśokan-Brāhmī, Kuṣāṇa-Brāhmī and Gupta-Brāhmī. Whereas the Aśokan-Brāhmī is plain, the Kuṣāṇa-Brāhmī develops angularities and the Gupta-Brāhmī develops curvatures. Inscriptions dating prior to the Christian Era are in the Aśokan-Brāhmī, those of first to third century AD are in the Kuṣāṇa-Brāhmī and those of fourth to sixth century AD are in the Gupta-Brāhmī. In adducing the date of a record it would not be proper only to compare its style of scribing with some record found at a distant site. The internal evidence of the record itself should also be looked into to determine its date.

Appendix I

खारवेल के हाथीगुम्फा लेख के संशोधित पाठ की नागरी लिपि में अनुकृति

{उन भग्नांशों के पाठ जो पढ़े जा सकते हैं ( ) में दिये गये हैं तथा उन भग्नांशों के संभावित एवं प्रस्तावित पाठ जो मिट चुके हैं [ ] में दिये गये हैं।}

पंक्ति १ नमो अरहंतानं (।) नमो सव-सिधानं (॥) ऐरेन महाराजेन महामेघवाहनेन चेति-राजव(–)स-वधनेन पसथ-सुभ-लखनेन चतुरंत-लुठण-गुण-उपेतेन कलिंगाधिपतिना सिरि-खारवेलेन

२ पंदरस-वसानि सिरि-कडार-सरीर-वता कीडिता कुमार-कीडिका (।) ततो लेख-रूप-गणना-ववहार-विधि-विसारदेन सव-विजावदातेन नव-वसानि योवरज (–) पसासितं (।) संपुण-चतुवीसति-वसो तदानि वधमान-सेस-योवनाभिविजयो ततिये-

३ कलिंग-राजवंसे-पुरिसयुगे महाराजाभिसेचनं पापुनाति (।) अभिसितमतो च पधमे वसे वात-विहत-गोपुर-पाकार-निवेसनं पटिसंखारयति कलिंग-नगरि-खिबीरं सितल-तडाग-पाडियो च बंधायति सवूयान-पटिसंथपनं च

४ कारयति पनतीसाहि-सत-सहसेहि (,) पकतियो च रंजयति (।) दुतिये च वसे अचितयिता सातकंनिं पछिम-दिसं हय-गज-नर-रध बहुलं-दंडं पठापयति कंहबेंना-गताय च सेनाय वितासिति असिक-नगरं (।) ततिये पुन वसे

५ गंधव-वेद-बुधो दप-नत-गीत-वादित-संदंसनाहि उसव-समाज-कारापनाहि च कीडपयति नगरिं (।) तथा चवुथे वसे विजाधराधिवासं अहत-पुव-कलिंग-पुवराज (ि) नव (`) (ि)स (ि) त . . . वितध-मकुट-सबिल(धि)ते च निखित-छत-

६ भिंगारे हित-रतन-सापतेये सव-रठिक-भोजके पादे वंदापयति (।) पंचमे च दानी वसे नंदराज-ति-वस-सत-ओघाटितं तनुसुलियवाटा-पणाडिं नगरं पवेसयति स . . . (।) अभिसितो च [छठे वसे] राजसेयं-संदसयंतो सवकर-वण-

७ अनुगह-अनेकानि सत-सहसानि विसजति पोर-जानपदं (।) सतमे च वसे पसासतो वजिरघरवति-घुसित-घरिनि* स(।) मतुक-पद पुंन[?दिया] त पा[पुनाति] (।) अठमे च वसे महता-सेनाय (अपति)हत-(भि)ति-गोरधगिरिं

८ घातापयिता राजगह-नप(⁻̇) पीडपयति (।) एतिनं च कंमपदान-पनादेन संबित-सेनावाहने विपमु(⁻̇)चितु मधुरं अपयातो यमना-[नदीं] . . . [सवर-राजान च] . . . . गछति) (।) पलवभार-

९ कपरुख-हय-गज-रध-सह यंते सव-घरावास(ी)-पूजि[त]-ठ (ॢ) [प]-[पूजा]य सव-गहनं च कारयितुं बमणानं जातिं परिहारं ददाति (,) अरहत च [पूजति (।) नवमे च वसे] सुविजय

१० ते उभय-प्राची-तटे राज-निवासं महाविजय-पासादं कारयति अठतिसाय-सत-सहसेहि (।) दसमे च वसे दंड-संधी-सा(म)मयो भरदवस-पठानं मह(ी)-जयनं . . . . कारापयति (।) [एकदसमे च वसे] प(।)यातानं मनि-रतनानि-सह याति

११ [दखिन दिसं] (मंदं) च अव-राज-निवेसितं पिथुडं गदभ-नगलेन कासयति (,) जनपद-भावनं च तेरस-वस-सत-कतं भिंदति तमिर-दह-संघातं (।) बारसमे च वसे . . . . स(ह)सेहि वितासयतो उतरापध-राजानो

१२ . . . मागधानं च विपुलं भयं जनेतो हथसं गंगाय पाययति (,) मागध (⁻̇) च राजानं बह(स)तिमितं पादे वंदापयति (,) नंदराज-नीतं च कालिंग-जिनं संनिवेस (`) [पूजयति] (,) [कोसात] (गह)-रत (नाि) न पडीहारेहि अंग-मगध-वसुं च नेयाति (।)

१३ ......क(`)तु (⁻̇) जठर-लखिल-(गो)पुरानि-सिहरानि निवेसयति सत-विसिकानं परिहारेहि (।) अभुतमछरियं च हथि-नाव-नीतं परिहरति...... हय-हथि-रतन-मानिको पंड-राजा (चेदानि अनेकानि) मुत-मणि-रतनानि आहरापयति इध सत-स[हसानि]

१४ [पंड-जनपद-वा]सिनो वसीकरोति (।) तेरसमे च वसे सुपवत-विजय-चके-कुमारी-पवते अरहते पखिण-संसितेहि काय-निसीदीयाय (।) यापुजवकेहि राज-भतिन(।) चिन-वतान(।) वस-सितान(।) पूजानुरत-उवासग-खारवेल-सिरिना जीव-देह-(सिरिता) परिखाता (।)

१५ [निमंतितेन राजा सिरि-खारवेलेन] सुकत-समण-सुविहितानं च सवदिसानं जनिनं तपसि-इसिनं संघयनं अरहत-निसीदीया समीपे पाभारे वराकार-समुथापिताहि अनेक-योजनाहिताहि [पनतिसतेहि] . . . सिलाहि सिंहपथ-रजी-सिंधुलाय निसयानि (।)

* अथवा, "वजिरघर-खतिय(।)-स(ि)त-घरिनि"

१६ . . . पटलके चतरे च वेडूरिय-गभे-थभे पतिठापयति (,) पानतरिय-सठ-सत-(व)सेहि मुखिय-कल-वोछिनं च चोयठ-अंगं संतिकं तुरियं उपादयति (।) खेम-राजा स वध-राजा स भिखु-राजा धम-राजा पसंतो सुनंतो अनुभवंतो कलाणानि (।)

१७ [पानतरिय-पनतिसत-वस ।] गुण-विसेस-कुसलो सव-पासंड-पूजको सव-देवायतन-संखारकारको अपतिहत-चक-वाहन-बलो चक-धरो गुत-चको पवत-चको राजसि-वंस-कुल-विनिशितो महाविजयो राजा-खारवेल-सिरि (।)

अशोक के भाब्रू लेख के अनुमोदित पाठ की नागरी लिपि में अनुकृति

पंक्ति १ पियदसि लाजा मागधे संघं अभिवादनं
आहा अपाबाधतं च फासु विहालतं चा (।)

२ विदिते वे भंते आवतके हमा बुधसि
धंमसि संघसीति गलवे चं पसादे च (।)
ए केंचि भंते

३ भगवता बुधेन भासिते सवे से सुभासिते
वा ए चु खो भंते हमियाये दिसेया हेवं
सधंमे

४ चिलठितीके होसतीति अलहां हकं तं वतवे (।)
इमां भंते धंमपलियायानि विनयसमुकसे

५ अलियवसानि अनागतभयानि मुनिगाथा
मोनेयसूते उपतिसपसिने ए चे लाघुलो-

६ वादे मुसावादं अधिगिच्य भगवता बुधेन
भासिते (।) एतां भंते धंमपलियायानि
इछामि

७ किंति बहुके भिखुपाये चा भिखुनिये चा
अभिखिनं सुनयु चा उपधालेयेयु च

८ हेवमेवा उपासका चा उपासिका चा (।)
एतें भंते इमं लिखापयामि अभिहेतं म
जानंत ति (।)

Appendix II

हाथीगुम्फा लेख के संशोधित पाठ का हिन्दी रूपान्तर कोष्ठक ( ) में पूरक शब्द हैं और [ ] में संभावित पाठों के अर्थ हैं।

"अरहंतों को नमस्कार हो।
सब सिद्धों को नमस्कार हो ।।

कलिंग के अधिपति, चेति राजवंश की कीर्ति को बढ़ाने वाले, प्रशस्त शुभ लक्षणों से भूषित और चारों दिगन्तों में विख्यात गुणों से अलंकृत आर्य महाराज महामेघवाहन श्री खारवेल द्वारा पन्द्रह वर्ष तक, जबकि उनका शरीर सुन्दर और कडार वर्ण का था, राजकुमारों के उपयुक्त क्रीड़ायें की गईं ।

तत्पश्चात् राजकीय लेख पद्धति, मुद्रा शास्त्र, लेखा शास्त्र, प्रशासकीय नियमों और अधिनियमों में निष्णात होकर और विद्या के सभी अंगों का ज्ञान प्राप्त करके उनके द्वारा नौ वर्ष तक युवराज के पद से शासन किया गया।

तब चौबीस वर्ष की अवस्था पूर्ण करने पर कलिंग के राजवंश की तीसरी पीढ़ी में, वह अपना महाराज्याभिषेक कराते हैं ताकि अपने शेष यौवन को विजयों द्वारा समृद्ध कर सकें।

और राज्याभिषेक होने के बाद प्रथम वर्ष में पैंतीस लाख (मुद्रा) व्यय करके वह कलिंग की राजधानी में तूफान से क्षतिग्रस्त गोपुरों, प्राकारों और निवासों की मरम्मत कराते हैं, शीतल तड़ाग के बाँध को सुदृढ़ कराते हैं और सब ही उद्यानों का प्रति-संस्थापन कराते हैं, और प्रजा का रंजन करते हैं।

और द्वितीय वर्ष में शातकर्णि की चिन्ता न करके वह अश्वारोही, हाथी, पदाति और रथ से समन्वित विपुल सैन्य पश्चिम दिशा में पठाते हैं और सेना के कृष्णवेणा नदी पर पहुँच जाने पर असिकों की राजधानी को त्रस्त करते हैं।

फिर तृतीय वर्ष में गंधर्व विद्या में प्रबुद्ध वह लोक-नृत्य, शास्त्रीय नृत्य, सुगम संगीत और वाद्य संगीत के कार्यक्रम कराके और विविध उत्सव और मेले कराके नगरवासियों का मनोविनोद करते हैं।

एवं चतुर्थ वर्ष में वह विद्याधरों के आवास (= विंध्याचल) में, जिसे कलिंग का कोइ भूतपूर्व राजा आहत न कर सका था, निवास करते हैं और सभी रठिकों और भोजकों से जिनके मुकुट और अलंकृत अश्व नष्ट कर दिये गये, छत्र और भृंगार निक्षिप्त कर दिये गये और रत्न एवं धन अपहृत कर लिये गये, अपने चरणों की वंदना कराते हैं।

और पंचम शुभ वर्ष में १०३वें वर्ष में राजा नन्द द्वारा उद्घाटित तनसुलियवाटा-प्रणाली (= नहर) को......सहस्र (मुद्रा) व्यय करके वह राजधानी में प्रवेश कराते हैं।

तथा राज्याभिषेक के छठे वर्ष में राज्य के ऐश्वर्य के प्रदर्शन हेतु वह सभी राज्य कर माफ कर देते हैं और नगर एवं ग्राम निवासियों पर लाखों मुद्राओं के मूल्य के अन्य अनेकों अनुग्रह विसर्जित करते हैं।

और जब वह सप्तम वर्ष में शासन कर रहे थे तो [पुण्य के उदय से] उनकी वजिरघरवती नाम की ग्रहिणी ने माता का पद प्राप्त किया।

एवं अष्टम वर्ष में अप्रतिहत भित्ति वाले गोरथगिरि का घात करके राजगृह के राजा को वह पीड़ा पहुँचाते हैं। और इस पराक्रम के कार्य की परम्परा में मथुरा को विमुक्त कराते हुए वह अपने सैन्य-वाहन सहित......यमुना [नदी] पहुँच जाते हैं। [तथा सभी अधीनस्थ राजाओं को साथ लेकर चलते हैं] पल्लवभार से युक्त कल्पवृक्ष, अश्व-सैन्य, गज-सैन्य और रथ-सैन्य के साथ वह सब गृहस्थों द्वारा [पूजित स्तूप की पूजा करने के लिए] जाते हैं एवं सर्वग्रहण अनुष्ठान करने के लिए ब्राह्मणों की जाति को दान देते हैं, और अरहंत की [पूजा करते हैं]।

[तथा नवम वर्ष में] इस उत्तम विजय की (स्मृति हेतु) प्राची नदी के दोनों तटों पर वह महाविजय-प्रासाद नाम के राजमहल का अड़तीस लाख (मुद्रा) की लागत से निर्माण कराते हैं।

और दसवें वर्ष में दंड और संधि के स्वामी वह सम्पूर्ण पृथ्वी की विजय हेतु भारतवर्ष में प्रस्थान के लिए (तैयारी) कराते हैं।

[एवं ग्यारहवें वर्ष में] वह मणि और रत्नों के साथ [दक्षिण दिशा में] मंद गति से प्रयाण करते हैं और अव (आन्ध्र?) राजाओं के निवास पिथुंड नगर में गदहों के हल चलवाते हैं; तथा अपने राज्य के कल्याण की दृष्टि से ११३वें वर्ष में बने तमिल देशों के संघ को भेदते हैं।

और बारहवें वर्ष में सहस्रों (वीरों की सेना के साथ) [उत्तर की ओर प्रयाण करते हुए] वह उत्तरापथ के राजाओं को त्रस्त करते हैं और मगध वासियों के हृदय में विपुल भय पैदा करते हुए अपने हाथियों और घोड़ों को गंगा में पानी पिलाते हैं, तथा मगध के राजा वृहस्पतिमित्र से अपने चरणों की वंदना कराते हैं, नंद-राज द्वारा कलिंग से लायी गयी जिनेन्द्र की प्रतिमा की मन्दिर [में पूजा करते हैं, और राज

कोष से] गृह-रत्नों का अपहरण करके अंग और मगध का धन ले आते हैं। [वापस लौटने पर] दो सहस्र (मुद्रा) व्यय करके वह गोपुरों के सभी सुदढ़ शिखरों पर केतु लगवाते हैं और अद्‌भुत आश्चर्य का विषय है कि हाथी-सैन्य और नाव-सैन्य भेजकर वह पांड्य राजा के घोड़े, हाथी, रत्न और माण्क्यि . . . ले लेते हैं और वहाँ लाखों के मूल्य के अनेक मुक्ता, मणि और रत्नों का भी अपहरण करते हैं एवं [पांड्य जनपद के निवासियों को] वश में करते हैं।

तथा तेरहवें वर्ष में राजसी भक्त जिसने व्रतों का पालन किया है, जो दैवी शक्ति से सम्पन्न है और जिसका पूजा में अनुराग है ऐसे उपासक श्री खारवेल द्वारा, जिनका जीव अभी देहाश्रित है, विजय मंडल में स्थित कुमारी पर्वत नामक शुभ पर्वत पर पूजा के हेतु संसार-मुक्त अरहंतों की काय-निषिद्‌या का उत्खनन कराया गया।

[राजा श्री खारवेल के आमंत्रण पर] सब दिशाओं से आने वाले सुकृत और सुविहित श्रमण, ज्ञानी, तपस्वी-ऋषि और सभी संघों के नेता [जिनकी संख्या ३५०० थी], सिंहपथ वाली रानी सिंधुला की निसिया के पास शिला पर पर्वत शिखर पर अरहंत की निषिद्या के समीप वराकार में [एकत्र होते हैं]।

और [सभामण्डप के सामने] वह (अर्थात् खारवेल) वैडूर्य गर्भित चौमुखे स्तंभ की प्रतिष्ठा कराते हैं, एवं १६५वें वर्ष से व्युच्छिन्न होती हूई मुख्य ध्वनि के शान्तिदायी द्वादश अंगों का शीघ्र पाठ कराते हैं। ऐसे क्षमाशील, बुद्धिमान, भिक्षुवृत्ति और धार्मिक राजा कल्याणों (= कल्याणकारी श्रुत) से संबंधित प्रश्न करते हैं, उनका श्रवण करते हैं और उनका मनन करते हैं।

[३५५वाँ वर्ष।] विशेष गुणों में कुशल, सब धर्मों को पूजने वाले, सब देवमन्दिरों का संस्कार करने वाले, अप्रतिहत चक्रवाहिनी के स्वामी, विजय-चक्र को धारण करने वाले, राज्य के रक्षक, प्रवृत्त-चक्र के स्वामी, राजवंशों और कुलों के आश्रय, महाविजयी, राजा श्री खारवेल।"

भाब्रू लेख का हिन्दी रुपान्तर

"मगध-राज प्रियदर्शि संघ को अभिवादन करके और उनके स्वास्थ्य एवं कुशलता की कामना करके ऐसा कहते हैं :

भंते, आपको विदित है कि बुद्ध, धर्म और संघ में हमारा कितना आदर एवं श्रद्धा है।

भंते, भगवान् बुद्ध ने जो कुछ कहा है वह सभी सुभाषित है परन्तु भंते, सद्‌धर्म के चिरस्थायी होने के उद्देश्य से हम वह बताते हैं जो कुछ हमने (उनके वचनों में उत्कृष्ट) देखा है।

भंते, भगवान् बुद्ध द्वारा कहे हुए ये धर्म वचन विनयसमुकसे (=धम्मचक्क-पवत्तन सुत्त), अलियवसानि (=अरियवंस सुत्त), अनागतभयानि (=अनागतभयानि सुत्त), मुनिगाथा (=मुनि सुत्त), मोनेयसूते (=नालक सुत्त), उपतिसपसिने (=सारिपुत्त सुत्त), तथा भूठ बोलने के सम्बन्ध में लाघुलोवाद (=राहुलोवाद सुत्त) हैं।

भंते, मैं चाहता हूँ कि ये धर्म वचन अधिकांश भिक्षु एवं भिक्षुणी बार-बार सुनें और (उनका) मनन करें तथा उसी प्रकार उपासक एवं उपासिका भी (करें)।

भंते, मैं इसे इसीलिये लिखा रहा हूँ कि वे (उक्त भिक्षु, भिक्षुणी, उपासक एवं उपासिका) मेरा अभिप्राय जान लें।"

Appendix III

Additional Notes

Himavanta-Therāvalī — Era of the dates — Date of the Buddha's *parinirvāṇa* — Date of Mahāvīra's *nirvāṇa* — Asikanagara and Kaṁhabeṁnā — Coyaṭha — Satakaṁnim̐ and Bahasatimita — Kaliṁga Jina — Schism and Khāravela — The Schism — Kaliṅga and Jainism — Nandas and Jainism — Aśoka and Kaliṅga

Himavanta-Therāvalī

In his letter dated 12–4–1930, published in the *Anekānta*, I, 6-7 (p. 351), Muni Jina Vijaya categorically stated that on a very careful reading he found the entire *Himavanta-Therāvalī* to be a work of fiction. It would be relevant to quote him *in extenso*:

> यह थेरावली अहमदाबाद में पण्डित–प्रवर श्री सुखलाल जी के प्रबन्ध से हमारे पास आ गई थी और उसका हमने खूब सूक्ष्मता के साथ वाचन किया। पढ़ने के साथ ही हमें वह सारा ही ग्रन्थ बनावटी मालूम हो गया और किसने और कब यह गढ़ डाला उसका भी कुछ हाल मालूम हो गया। इन बातों के विशेष उल्लेख की मैं अभी आवश्यकता नहीं समझता। सिर्फ इतना ही कह देना उचित होगा कि हिमवन्त–थेरावली के कल्पक ने, खारवेल के लेख वाली जो किताब हमारी (*प्राचीन जैनलेखसंग्रह*, प्रथम भाग) छपाई हुई है और जिसमें पं भगवानलाल इन्द्रजी के पढ़े हुए लेख का पाठ और विवरण दिया गया है उसी किताब को पढ़कर, उस पर से यह थेरावली का वर्णन बना लिया है। उस कल्पक को श्री जायसवाल जी के पाठ की कोई कल्पना नहीं हुई थी इसलिये उस कल्पक की थेरावली अप–टु–डेट नहीं बन सकी। खैर। ऐसी रीति हमारे

यहाँ बहुत प्राचीन काल से चली आ रही है इससे इसमें हमें कोई आश्चर्य पाने की बात नहीं।

[This *Therāvalī* was received by me through the good offices of Pandit-pravar Sri Sukhlal ji in Ahmedabad and I went through it very thoroughly. On reading it I found the entire book to be a work of fiction and also came to know of something as to who invented it and when. I do not deem it necessary now to specially mention that. Only this much would be proper to say that the fictionist of the *Himavanta-Therāvalī* invented the narrative of the *Therāvalī* on reading the Khāravela's inscription in my book *Prācīna Jaina Lekha Saṁgraha*, part I, wherein is given the text of the inscription as read by Pt. Bhagwanlal Indraji. The *Therāvalī* of that fictionist could not be made up-to-date as he could not divine the reading of Sri Jayaswal ji. Anyway. There is nothing to wonder in it because this practice is continuing with us from very old times.]

Pt. Sukhlal was an eminent Śvetāmbara scholar. Muni Jina Vijaya was himself a Śvetāmbara Muni but he was also an unbiased scholar and an eminent archaeologist who would not be influenced by sectarian prejudice and be a party to distorting the source material. He had himself worked on the Hāthīgumphā Inscription with K.P. Jayaswal.

On Muni Jina Vijaya's finding that the *Himavanta-Therāvalī* was not an authentic work, the scholars (Jayaswal, Banerji, Barua and Sircar) who had worked so hard on this inscription, did not take any notice of it. Muni Kalyana Vijaya and Muni Punya Vijaya had tried to project it as a valuable source, but they did not pursue the matter after the categorical finding given by Muni Jina Vijaya.

After some 45 years Acharya Śrī Hastimala ji Maharaja revived this *Therāvalī* as an important source in his *Jainadharma kā Maulika Itihāsa*. It is now creating confusion and misleading the scholars who are not aware of Muni Jina Vijaya's finding.

A curious fact about this *Therāvalī* has been noted by Dr. Sagarmal Jain as late as 1994 that its original has not been available since its translation into Gujarati and its Gujarati translation by Pt. Hiralal Hansraj of Jamnagar is the only evidence of its existence (*Sāgara Jaina-Vidyā Bhāratī*, pt. I, p. 267 fn. 36). Hastimala ji seems to have used the original manuscript because he quotes the Prakrit text and gives the source as *Himavanta Sthavirāvali hastalikhita* (*op. cit.*, pt. II, pp. 476-94). It is to be specially noted that the impugned text has never been published and possibly it does not exist now.

Era of the dates

Sten Konow also thought that the dates given in the Hāthīgumphā Inscription were connected with the Mahāvīra Era (*Acta Orientalia*, I). N.S. Ramaswami also upholds this view (*J.O.R.*, XXXVIII, p. 36).

Date of the Buddha's parinirvāṇa

M. Winternitz also notes that "all the seemingly convincing evidence which we thought we had acquired in favour of various dates between 477 and 487 BC, has in every case proved to be uncertain and doubtful" (*History of Indian Literature,* II, p. 597).

A.B. Keith also finds the usual dating 487-477 BC uncertain and says that "the case against the traditional date is insufficient to justify its rejection out and out" (*Buddhist Philosophy in India and Ceylon*, p. 32).

Even as late as April 1988 it emerged at a symposium held at the Academie der Wissenschaften (Gottingen, Germany) that the general agreement among scholars that the Buddha died within a few years of 480 BC, had become a thing of the past (ref. *When did the Buddha Live*?, ed. Heinz Bechert, 1995).

V.A. Smith, E.J. Thomas, G.P. Malasekhara, Mrs. Rhys Davids, Radha Kumud Mookerji and K.P. Jayaswal already support the traditional date of 544 BC for the Buddha's *parinirvāṇa* (demise).

Date of Mahāvīra's nirvāṇa

An entirely new chronological build-up is being suggested by some scholars and it has been summarised in a way in *The Mahāvīra Era* supplement appended to the *Tulsī Prajñā*, XVIII, 4 (28 February, 1993). It has been edited by Dr. Parmeshwar Solanki who himself pushes the date of Mahāvīra's *nirvāṇa* back to 1761 BC and includes an article by Upendra Nath Roy who pushes the date further back to 1834 BC. They respectively place the demise of the Buddha in 1738 BC and 1890 BC. They substantiate their view by an amalgam of Kalki myth of the Jains, *Saptarṣi* (Seven Star) constellation, and the lore in the *Vāyu*, *Matsya* and *Viṣṇu* Purāṇas. In their zeal to press their point, Roy would dismiss the epigraphic evidence dateable in 396 BC affirming the 544 BC date of the Buddha's demise (ref. Dr. S. Parana Vitana: 'New Light on the Buddhist Era in Ceylon and Early Simhalese Chronology', *University of Ceylon Review*, XVIII, 1960, pp. 19-55), while Solanki would invent *dasame ca vase Kaliṁga rājavasāne tatiyayuge sagāvasāne Kaliṁgayuvarājanaṁ vāsakāraṁ kārāpayati* as the tenth line of the Hāthīgumphā Inscription of Khāravela. All this pushes the chronology of the historical period of Ancient India also into a mythological haze, and these dates ought not to be taken seriously therefore.

Similarly, some scholars insist on 467 BC as the date of Mahāvīra's *nirvāṇa* (demise) on the basis of some Śvetāmbara Paṭṭāvalis including the *Himavanta-Therāvalī* and the error made by Hemacandra Sūri in placing Candragupta 155 years after Mahāvīra's *nirvāṇa*. Dr. Sagarmal Jain admits that the authenticity of the dates of pontiffs given in the Paṭṭāvalis is suspect and there is no basis to reconcile the discrepencies, but all the same he would insist on 467 BC (*vide, Sāgara Jaina-Vidyā Bhāratī,* pt. I, pp. 254-68). It is to be noted that the error of Hemacandra was detected by Merutuṅga in his *Vicāraśreṇī*, and that Hemacandra himself did not have any doubt about 527 BC as the date of Mahāvīra's *nirvāṇa* since he says in his

Triṣaṣṭiśalākāpuruṣacarita, X.12.45-46, that Kumārapāla will be the king 1669 years after the *nirvāṇa*, *i.e.*, in AD 1142, the otherwise well-known date of Kumārapāla's accession.

Asikanagaraṁ and Kaṁhabeṁnā in L 4

Dr. M.K. Dhavalikar prefers *Musikanagaraṁ* to *Asikanagaraṁ* and identifies it with Maski in Raichur district *(A.B.O.R.I*, LIII, p. 289). Dr. V.V. Mirashi, however, points out that Asika is mentioned with Asmaka in the list of territories in the Nasik Cave Inscription of Year 19 of the Sātavāhana Vāśiṣṭhiputra Pulumāvi and that the Asika region seems to be identical with Khandesh which is in accord with the geographical direction given by Khāravela. (*Sātavāhanon aur Paścimī Kṣatrapon kā Itihāsa*, p. 78).

N.S. Ramaswami prefers to identify *Kaṁhabeṁnā* with the R. Krishna particularly in the light of the Guntupille Inscription (*J.O.R.*, XXXVIII, p. 36). But the difficulty in this identification is that the Krishna flows to the south of the Kaliṅga and not to its west.

Coyaṭha in L 16

The reading has been consistently *coyaṭha* but it has been sought to be equated with *cosaṭha* to mean 'sixty-four'. This equation is not sustainable because neither in this inscription nor otherwise in Prakrit *ya* is interchangeable with *sa*. 'Four Eight' appears to be a poetic way of saying 'twelve' (*dvādaśa*) instead of using the prosaic *bārasa*. *Bārasa* is used for '12' in L 11.

Sātakaṁniṁ and Bahasatimita

Dr. V.V. Mirashi also holds that Sātakaṁniṁ, the powerful adversary of Khāravela, was Śātakarṇi, the third king of the Sātavāhana dynasty who ruled for 10 years after 41 years of the founding of the dynasty by Simuka (*op. cit.*, pp. 80-81).

He also thinks that when Khāravela invaded Magadha, no Śuṅga king ruled there but Bṛhaspatimitra of the Mitra dynasty ruled. He is also of the view that there is no basis for holding the view that the Śuṅga, Kaṇva and Āndhra (Sātavāhana) kings ruled from Pāṭaliputra (*op. cit.*, pp. 75-78).

This, in essence, supports my discussion.

Kaliṁga Jina

The anthropomorphic image of the deity evolved in about first century BC and it took about 500 years to fully develop at Mathura as evidenced by the finds there. But the torsos found at Lohanipur, one of which may be the Kaliṁga Jina, indicate that there was a school of sculpture in eastern India also where the anthropomorphic image emerged independently and earlier, too. However, not much is known about this school in the absence of any finds besides the lone torsos from Lohanipur.

It is evident from the text of the inscription that the image was taken as a war trophy, but not without reverence, by the Nanda king to his capital Pāṭaliputra where he installed it in a temple, and that Khāravela had worshipped it in that temple. There is no mention that he carried it back to Kaliṅga. In fact, as a worshipful lay-devotee he would not think of desecrating the temple where the image was already being worshipped.

It is to be noted that the early anthropomorphic nudes from Mathura, as well as from eastern India, represented the Arahaṁta Jina and did not signify any particular of the 24 Tīrthaṅkaras unless the name was mentioned in the inscription on the pedestal. The distinguishing *lāñchana*s (symbols), and other iconographic details, developed much later from the 5th century AD onwards. Therefore, it would be just hazardous to say that the Kaliṅga Jina, or either of the torsos, is an icon of R̥ṣabhanātha, Śītalanātha or Mahāvīra, respectively the 1st, 10th and 24th Tīrthaṅkara.

Schism and Khāravela

The Buddhist tradition is candid in admitting that Gautama

the Buddha had to face dissidence in his life-time; his cousin Devadatta and his own disciples in the Ghositārāma at Kauśāmbī were the trouble shooters. Among the Jains the Digambara tradition does not refer to any dissidence in the life time of Mahāvīra, but the Śvetāmbara tradition refers to the emergence of dissidence in the fourteenth and sixteenth years of his ministry. However, the final schism into the Digambara and Śvetāmbara was finalised some 600 years after Mahāvīra (ref. Dr. Hiralal Jain: *Bhāratīya Saṁskriti mein Jaina Dharma kā Yogadāna*, pp. 30-31).

There is nothing in the inscription of Khāravela to suggest that he supported any of the dissident factions that may have existed in his time. The term *Saṁghayana* seems to suggest that there were several groups of monks under their respective leaders. The purpose of the Council was obviously to consolidate the extant canonical knowledge as might have been preserved by the different *saṁgha*s or groups of monks. Nothing beyond that can be inferred from the text of the inscription.

The Schism

The schism in Jainism was formalised in *circa* AD 79-82 as the Digambara and the Śvetāmbara. The major doctrinal differences can be summed up as *Strī-mukti* and *Kevali-bhukti*, and the patent appearence of the monks as nude and covered. The Digambara doctrine would not allow a woman to attain salvation and, also, would not think it necessary to take food after attaining the Supreme Knowledge (*kaivalya*). The Śvetāmbara doctrine does not object to either and proclaims that Malli, the 19th Tīrthaṅkara, was a woman. Further, Mahāvīra of the Śvetāmbaras preaches by word of mouth, but he of the Digambaras utters only a sound (*divya dhvani*) which is interpreted by the Gaṇadharas, all the 11 of whom were Brahmins.

When the two factions parted company finally towards the close of the first century AD, some 600 years after the demise of

Mahāvīra, the monks donning white robe got the nomenclature Śvetāmbara (the White Robed); later on some other colours were also added.

In course of time the sectarian differences became so prominent that the Digambaras declared the first 11 Aṅgas as lost because the Śvetāmbaras claimed to preserve them, and *vice versa* the Śvetāmbaras treated the 12th Aṅga as lost because the Digambaras claimed to preserve its knowledge. Further, they made different life stories of the Tīrthaṅkaras so-much-so as altering the fact and place of birth, time and place of First Sermon and even the timing and spot of *nirvāṇa* of Mahāvīra; began spelling the names of holy places differently (*e.g.*, Sammed-Shikharji and Sammet-Shikharji); started observing the *parva* (holy days) on different days and in different ways; and rendered even the *maṅgala-śloka* differently: the Digambara saying —

Maṅgalam Bhagavān Vīro, Maṅgalam Gautamo Gaṇi.
Maṅgalam Kundakundādyā, Jainadharmostu maṅgalam.

while the Śvetāmbara would say —

Maṅgalam Bhagavān Vīro, Maṅgalam Gautamo Prabhuḥ.
Maṅgalam Sthūlibhadrādyā, Jainadharmostu maṅgalam.

Kaliṅga and Jainism

According to the Jain puranic tradition, R̥ṣabhadeva, the first Tīrthaṅkara, is said to have named a region Kaliṅga after the name of one of his 100 sons to whom that region was bequeathed. But it is not possible to infer the geographical situation of that Kaliṅga.

The coastal tract along the Bay of Bengal between the rivers Damodar and Godavari, has been known as Kaliṅga in the historical times. Its association with Jainism dates back to nearly 28 centuries. Karakaṇḍu, originally a prince of Campā (in Bihar) and later a king of Kaliṅga, is said to have been a follower of Pārśvanātha (*nirvāṇa circa* 777 BC), the 23rd Tīrthaṅkara. Thereafter, a sister of Siddhārtha, the father of

Mahāvīra (the 24th Tīrthaṅkara), is said to have been married to Jitaśatru, King of Kaliṅga. Jitaśatru is also said to have offered the hand of his daughter Yaśodā to Prince Mahāvīra. The Digambara tradition denies marriage, but the Śvetāmbara tradition makes Mahāvīra not only marry Yaśodā but also to beget a daughter, Priyadarśanā by name, who was to marry Jamāli. Jamāli joined Mahāvīra's Order and, incidentally, he happened to be the first dissenter in the 14th year of Mahāvīra's ministry.

Jitaśatru was in all probability a follower of Jainism as his close relationship with Mahāvīra seems to indicate. It cannot be said that at the time of Nanda King's invasion of Kaliṅga, a hundred years later, the king was a descendent of Jitaśatru. But this much is confirmed by Khāravela's inscription that the personal faith of that royal family of Kaliṅga was Jainism because the Nanda King took away the Kaliṅga Jina (the image of Jina, Arahaṁta or Tīrthaṅkara, which was specially revered in Kaliṅga) as a war trophy.

Nandas and Jainism

The Nanda King took away the Kaliṅga Jina to Magadha and installed it in a temple where Khāravela himself worshipped it in his 12th regnal year (ref. L 12, p. 17 fn. 5, *supra*). It indicates that the Nanda King may have been an adherent of Jainism, otherwise he could have desecrated or destroyed the image. But his personal faith did not come in his way when dealing with statecraft, and he invaded and humiliated the Jain king of Kaliṅga for building up the Magadhan Empire

The tradition writers do not, however, appear to have done justice to the Nandas. The Brahmins made them Śūdra and the Buddhists called them *nāpita* (low caste of barber), because the Nandas did not subscribe to Brahmanism and Buddhism

Surprisingly the Jain tradition also does not call the Nandas, noble Kṣatriya, most probably because when the tradition was redacted it had been long forgotten that they were adherents of

Jainism and the general Brahmanical bias infected the Jain writers also.

Aśoka and Kaliṅga

Aśoka has himself left an account of his conquest of Kaliṅga in the eighth year of his reign in his Rock Edict XIII. His two Kaliṅga Edicts also bear on his concern for the conquered people of Kaliṅga. There is nothing to suggest that this conquest was to punish a king or people following a different religion. It was a conquest to annex Kaliṅga and thus extend the borders of his empire to the eastern coast. The difference between the campaigns of Nandarāja and Aśoka appears to be that while the former was a campaign of conquest and annexation, the latter was to bring it back under the imperial administration.

Aśoka adopted Buddhism as his personal faith more than a year after the conquest of Kaliṅga, and, therefore, it cannot be connected with his persecuting zeal for Buddhism. In the twelfth and nineteenth years of his reign he donated cave dwellings for the Ājīvakas. In all his edicts he mentions the Brahmins and the Śramaṇas together and in his Pillar Edict VII, recorded in the year 27 of his reign, he specifically mentions his concern for the welfare of the Buddhist Saṁgha, the Brahmins, the Ājīvakas and the Nirgranthas (*i.e.*, the Jain monks and their followers). The *dharma* or the code of conduct prescribed in his edicts is based on the moral principles for individual and social conduct aimed at harmony and tolerance among his subjects and with his neighbours.

Appendix IV

Chronology

544 BC	*Parinirvāṇa* of the Buddha; commencement of the Buddha Era
527 BC	*Nirvāṇa* of Mahāvīra; commencement of the Mahāvīra Era
467 BC (ME 60)	Commencement of the Nanda rule in Magadha and Ujjayinī
424 BC (ME 103)	Accession of Mahāpadma Nanda; conquest of Kaliṅga and inauguration of the Tanasuliyavāṭā canal by him
414 BC (ME 113)	Formation of the Tamila Confederacy
362 BC (ME 165)	Decline of the Principal Scripture of the Jains
324 BC	Accession of Candragupta Maurya in Magadha
317 or 312 BC (ME 210 or 215)	End of the Nanda rule and commencement of the Maurya rule in Ujjayinī; construction of the Sudarśana lake near Girnar
300 BC	Accession of Bindusāra
272 BC	Accession of Aśoka
260 BC	Promulgation of R.E. I-IV, M.R.E. I-II, and Barabar Cave Inscriptions of the Year 12
259 BC	Promulgation of R.E. V-XIV and K.R.E. I-II
253 BC	Barabar Cave Inscription of the Year 19
252 BC	Rummindei and Nigliva records
246 BC	P.E. I-VI, Schism Edicts, Queen's Edict and Bhabru Edict
245 BC	P.E. VII
236 BC	Death of Aśoka and disintegration of the Maurya Empire; founding of the Sātavāhana kingdom near Nasik

	and of the Cedi kingdom in Kaliṅga
219 BC	Death of Samprati and further dismemberment of the Maurya Empire; founding of independent kingdoms in Mathura, Ahicchatrā, and Kauśāmbī
209 BC	Birth of Khāravela
206 BC	End of the Maurya rule in Magadha and installation of Bahasatimita as the King of Magadha
206-172 BC	Bahasatimita in Magadha and Kauśāmbī
204-169 BC	Puṣyamitra Śuṅga in Vidiśā and Ujjayinī
194-184 BC	Śrī Śātakarṇi, third ruler of the Sātavāhana dynasty
194 BC	Khāravela associated in administration as *yuvarāja*
185 BC	Coronation of Khāravela as the King of Kaliṅga
185-172 BC	Khāravela in Kaliṅga
185-184 BC	Renovation of the capital
184-183 BC	Expedition in the west up to the R. Kṛṣṇaveṇā
183-182 BC	Musical parties, festivals and fairs in the capital
182-181 BC	Expedition in the Vindhyas and subjugation of the Raṭhikas and Bhojakas
181-180 BC	Tanasuliyavāṭā canal brought into the capital
180-179 BC	Display of opulence by remitting taxes and bestowing favours
179-178 BC	A child is born to Queen Vajiragharavatī
178-177 BC	Storming of Gorathagiri and liberation of Mathura; worship of the *stūpa* and performance of the Sarvagrahaṇa ceremony at Mathura
177-176 BC	Building of the Mahāvijayaprāsāda on the R. Prācī
176-175 BC	Preparations for the campaign of conquest
175-174 BC	Annihilation of Pithuṇḍa and breaking of the Tamila Confederacy
174-173 BC	Conquest of Magadha; worship of the Kaliṅga-Jina; fixing of pinnacles on the gates of the capital; and subjugation of the Pāṇḍya kingdom
173-172 BC	Excavation of the Relic Memorial on the Mt. Kumārī and convening of the Jain Council near that shrine
172 BC (ME 355)	Incising of the Hāthīgumphā Inscription

Appendix V

Transcription Chart of Brāhmī Script

Nagari	Roman	Brāhmī
VOWELS		
अ	**a**	𑀅, 𑀅
आ	**ā**	𑀆, 𑀆
इ	**i**	𑀇
उ	**u**	𑀉
ए	**e**	𑀏, 𑀏
ऐ	**ai**	𑀐, 𑀐
ओ	**o**	𑀑
अं	**ṁ**	𑀅𑀁, 𑀅𑀁
CONSONANTS		
क	**ka**	𑀓
ख	**kha**	𑀔, 𑀔
ग	**ga**	𑀕, 𑀕
घ	**gha**	𑀖, 𑀖
ङ	**ṅa**	𑀗
च	**ca**	𑀘, 𑀘

छ	**cha**	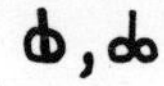
ज	**ja**	
झ	**jha**	
ञ	**ña**	
ट	**ṭa**	
ठ	**ṭha**	
ड	**ḍa**	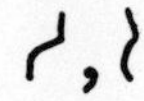
ढ	**ḍha**	
ण	**ṇa**	
त	**ta**	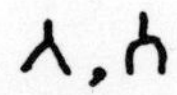
थ	**tha**	
द	**da**	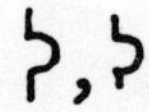
ध	**dha**	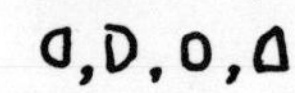
न	**na**	
प	**pa**	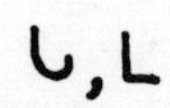
फ	**pha**	
ब	**ba**	
भ	**bha**	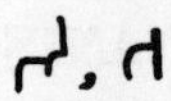
म	**ma**	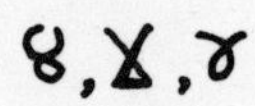
य	**ya**	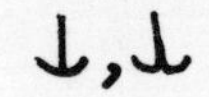
र	**ra**	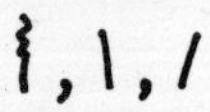
ल	**la**	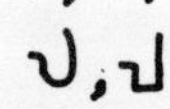
व	**va**	
श	**śa**	

ष ṣa

स sa

ह ha

MEDIALS

का kā

कि ki

की kī

कु ku

कू kū

के ke

को ko

कं kaṁ

खा khā

खि khi

खु khu

खे khe

खो kho

गी gī

गु gu

गो go

जा jā

जो ño

टा ṭā

टे ṭe

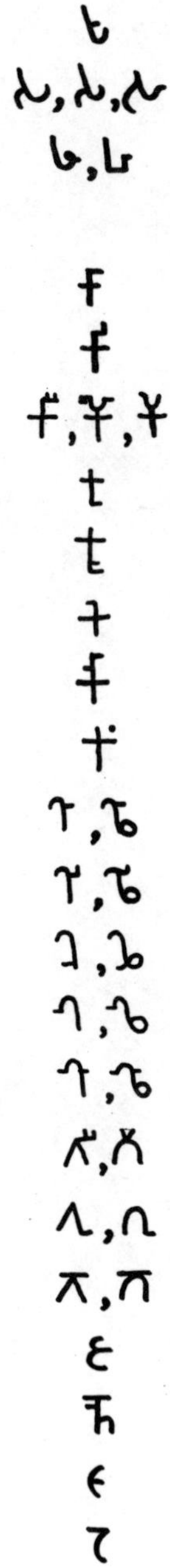

डु	**ḍu**
णा	**ṇā**
णो	**ṇo**
था	**thā**
थि	**thi**
थी	**thī**
थु	**thu**
थे	**the**
थो	**tho**
दीं	**dīṁ**
दु	**du**
धि	**dhi**
नु	**nu**
पु	**pu**
बा	**bā**
बि	**bi**
बी	**bī**
बु	**bu**
भिं	**bhiṁ**
मा	**mā**
मु	**mu**
मे	**me**
मो	**mo**
यु	**yu**

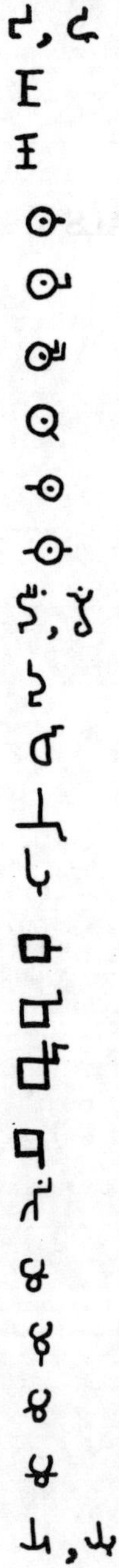

यू	**yū**	𑀬𑀽, 𑀬𑀽
यो	**yo**	𑀬𑁄, 𑀬𑁄
रि	**ri**	𑀭𑀺
री	**rī**	𑀭𑀻
रु	**ru**	𑀭𑀼
रो	**ro**	𑀭𑁄
लिं	**liṁ**	𑀮𑀺𑀁
ले	**le**	𑀮𑁂
शि	**śi**	𑀰𑀺
शो	**śo**	𑀰𑁄
MIXED CONSONANTS		
च्य	**cya**	𑀘𑁆𑀬
प्र	**pra**	𑀧𑁆𑀭

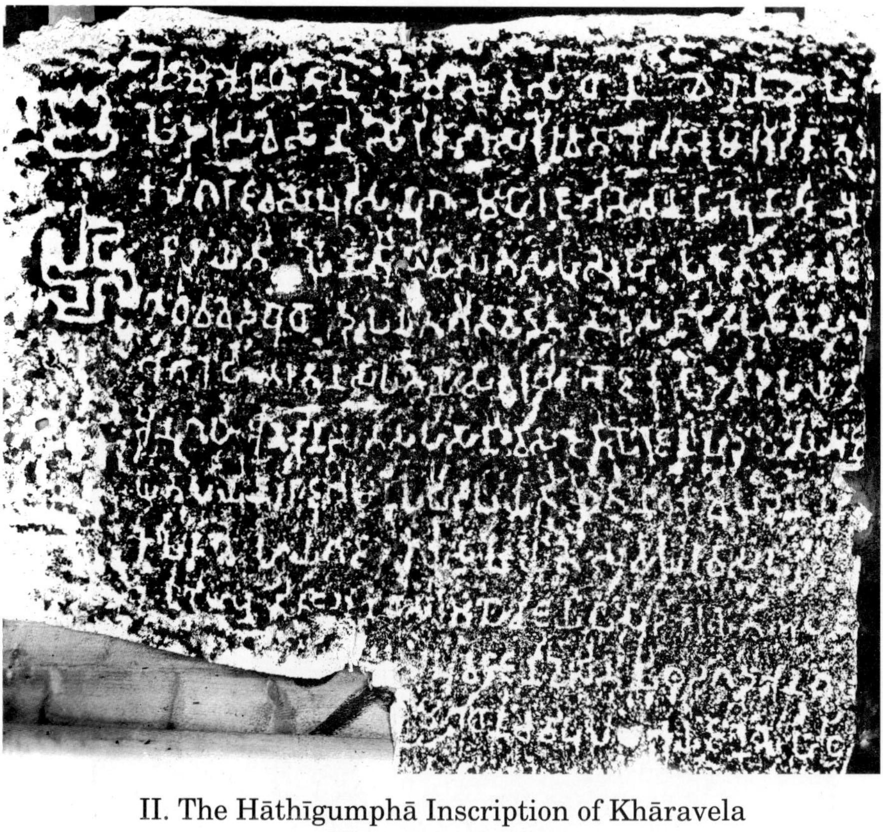

II. The Hāthīgumphā Inscription of Khāravela
(first part) L 1-12

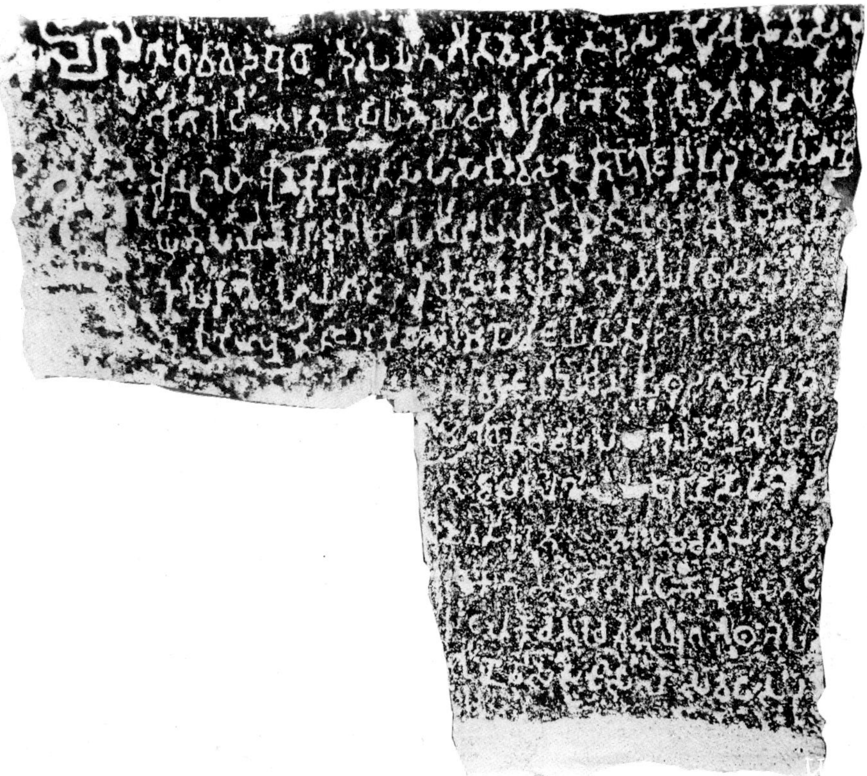

III. The Hāthīgumphā Inscription of Khāravela
(first part) L 5-17

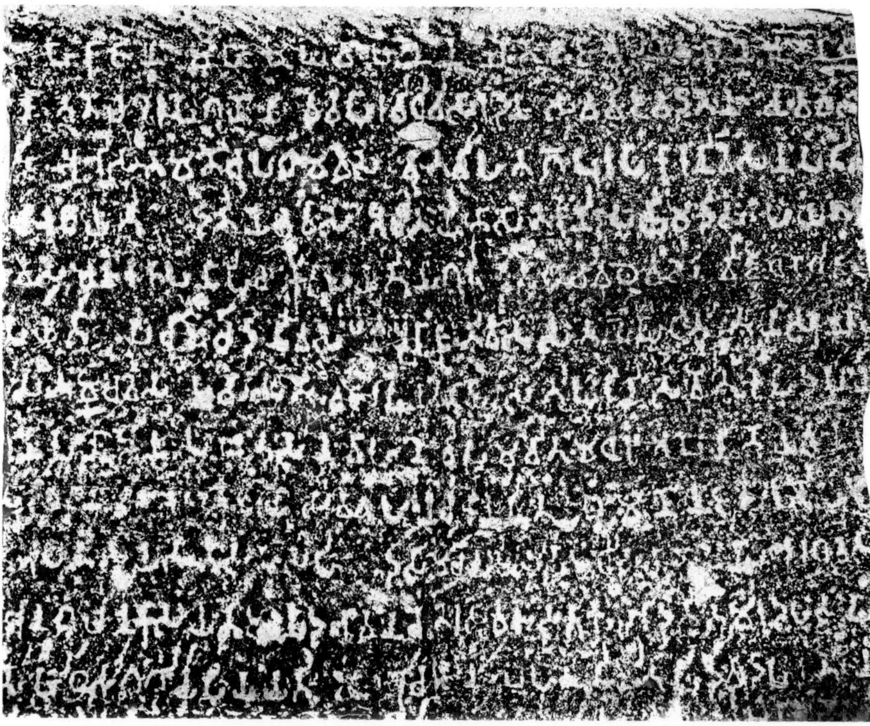

IV. The Hāthīgumphā Inscription of Khāravela
(second part) L 1-12

V. The Hāthīgumphā Inscription of Khāravela (second part) L 5-17

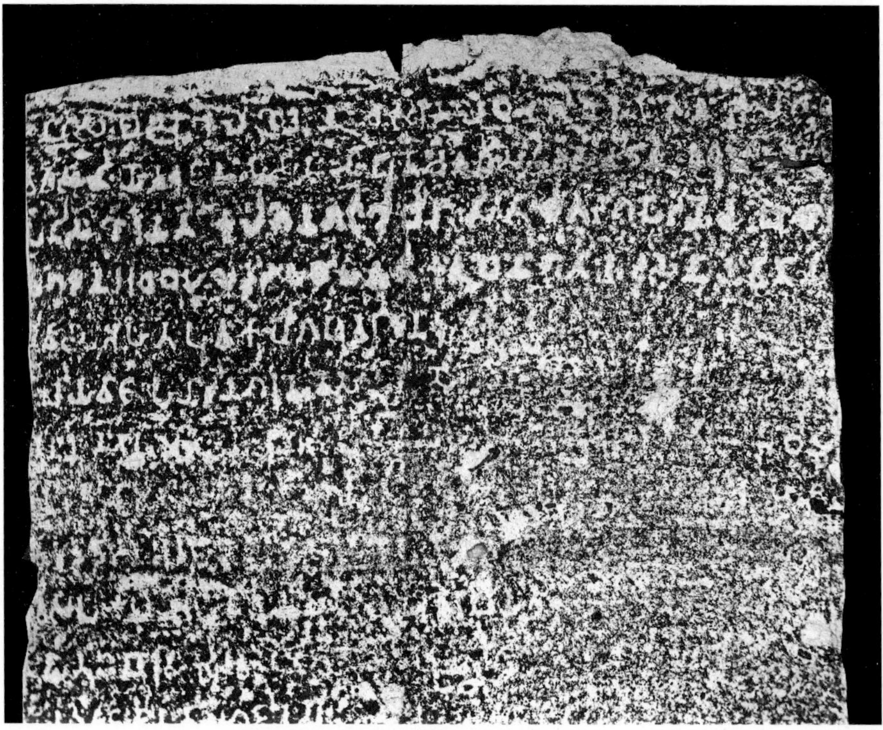

VI. The Hāthīgumphā Inscription of Khāravela
(third part) L 1-12

VII. The Hāthīgumphā Inscription of Khāravela (third part) L 5-17

VIII. The Hāthīgumphā Inscription of Khāravela
(fourth part) L 1-12 (concluded)

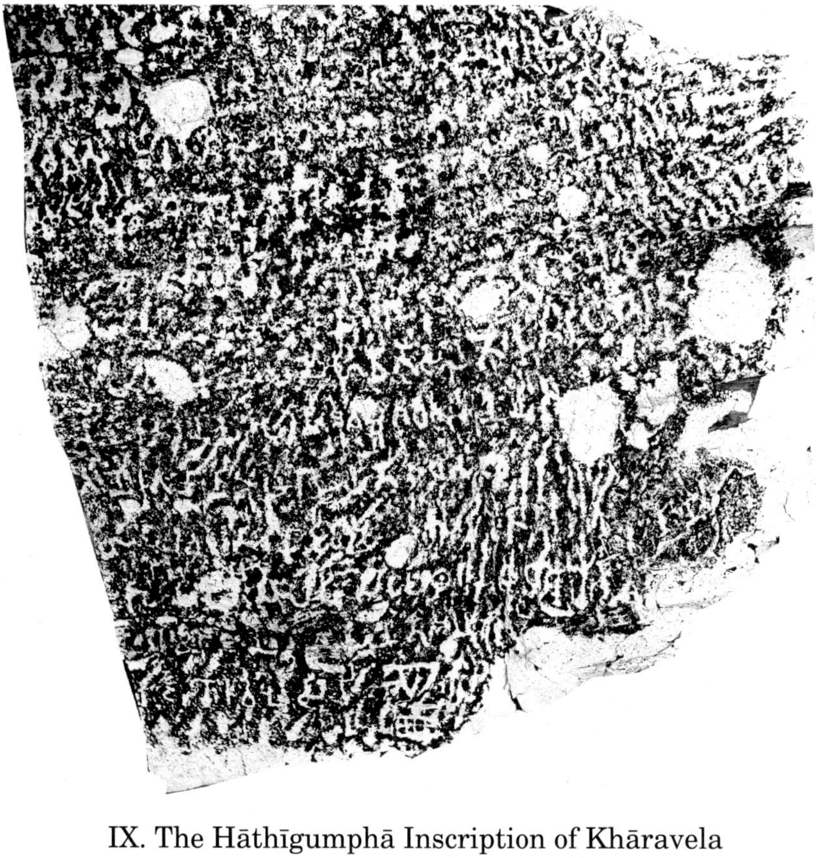

IX. The Hāthīgumphā Inscription of Khāravela
(fourth part) L 5-17 (concluded)

X. The Hāthīgumphā

XI. The Hāthīgumphā and other caves on the Udayagiri

XII. The remains of the apsidal structure overlying the Hāthīgumphā

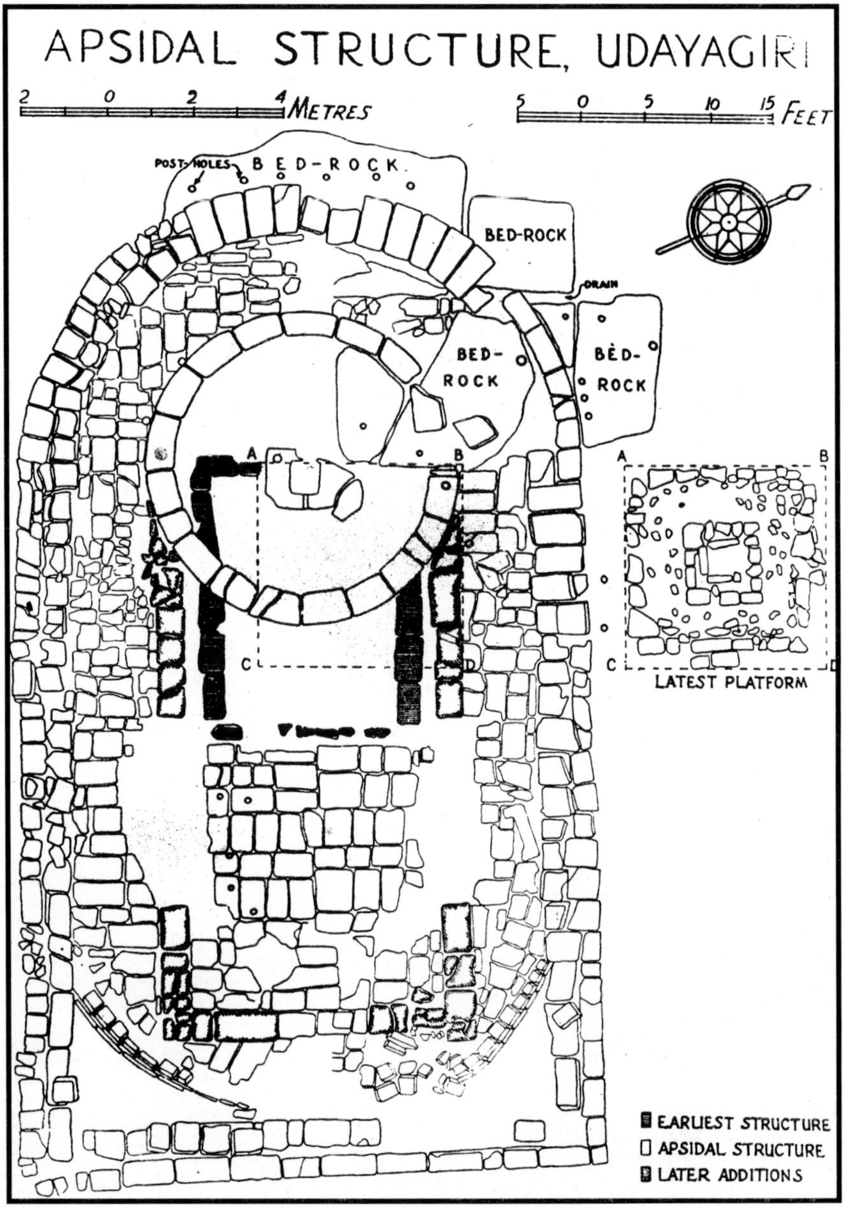

XIII. Sketch of the apsidal structure

XIV. The Mañcapurī and Svargapurī

XV. Worship scene on a frieze in the Mañcapurī

XVI. The Pātālapurī

XVII. The Rāṇī Gumphā

B. Prakrit

Bhagavatī Sūtra

Daṁsaṇasāra (Darśanasāra) of Devasena

Kunda-kunda Prābhṛta Saṁgraha (ed. K.C. Shastri)

Pannavanā Sūtra

Samavāyāṁga Sūtra

Ṣaṭkhaṇḍāgamaḥ (*Chakkhaṁḍagama*), ed. H.L. Jain & A.N. Upadhye, 1973

Sukhabodhā commentary of Devendragaṇin on the *Uttarajhayaṇa*

Tapāgaccha Paṭṭāvali

Ṭhānāṅga (*Sthānāṅga Sūtra*)

Uttarajhayaṇa (*Uttarādhyayana Sūtra*)

C. Pāli

Aṅguttara Nikāya

Cullavagga

Dīgha Nikāya

Itivuttaka

Jātaka, ed. V. Fausholl, III (Kumbhakāra Jātaka)

Mahāvyutpatti

Majjhima Nikāya

Sīgalovādasutta

Suttanipāta

Udāna

Vinaya-piṭakam

Visuddhimagga of Buddhaghosa

D. Apabhraṁśa

Karakaṁḍacariu, ed. H.L. Jain

II. MODERN WORKS

A. General Histories

A Comprehensive History of India, Vol. II —

The Muryas and Sātavāhanas — 325 BC-AD 300, ed. K.A. Nilakanta Sastri, 1957

Babylonion and Oriental Records, I

Cambridge History of India, Vol. I, ed. E.J. Rapson (Indian reprint, 1955)

The Age of the Nandas and Mauryas, ed. K.A. Nilakanta Sastri, 1952

The Early History of the Deccan, Pt. I-VI, ed. G. Yazdani, 1960

The History and Culture of the Indian People, Vol. II — *The Age of Imperial Unity,* ed. R.C. Majumdar & A.D. Pusalker (2nd edn., 1953)

B. Books and authors

Aiyanger, S.K., *Ancient India and South Indian History and Culture*, I

Allan, John, *British Museum Catalogue of Coins of Ancient India,* 1936

Bali, Chaṇdrakant, *Khāravela Praśasti, Punarmūlyāṁkana* (Hindi)

Banerji, R.D., *History of Orissa*, I, 1930

———, *The Palaeography of the Hāthīgumphā and Nānāghāṭ Inscriptions* (*M.A.S.B.*, *X*)

Barua, Dr. B.M., *Aśoka and His Inscriptions*, pt. I-II, 1946

———, *Old Brāhmī Inscriptions in the Udayagiri and Khaṇḍagiri Caves,* 1929

Bechert, Heinz (ed.), *When did the Buddha Live? The Controversy of the Dating of the Historical Buddha*, 1995

Bhandarkar, D.R., *Aśoka*, 3rd edn. 1955

Bhatt, Janardan, *Aśoka ke Dharmalekha*, Hindi, 1923

Bhattacharya, V., *Buddhist Texts recommended by Aśoka*, 1945 Brahmappa, G., *Samrāṭa Khāravela*, Kannad, fiction, 1964

Brown, Percy, *Indian Architecture* (*Buddhist and Hindu Periods*), 4th edn., 1959

Bühler, G., *On the Origin of the Indian Brāhmī Alphabet*, 2nd edn., 1898

Chakravartinayanar, A., *Pañcāstikāyasāra* (Intro., trans.),

———, *The Religion of Ahimsa* (*The Essence of Jaina Philosophy and Ethics*), 1957

Chatterji, S.K., *Indo-Aryan and Hindi*

Cunningham, A., *Corpus Inscriptionum Indicarum*, vol. I, 1877

Dani, A.H., *Indian Palaeography*

Dikshit, K.N., *Prehistoric Civilization of the Indus Valley*

Diringer, David, *The Alphabet*

Dutt, N., & Bajpai, K.D., *Development of Buddhism in Uttar Pradesh*, 1956

Eggermont, P.H.L., *The Chronology of the Reign of Asoka Moriya*, 1956

Eliot, Charles, *Hindusim and Buddhism*, 1921

Gerini, *Researches on Ptolemy*

Gode, P.K., and Karve, C.G., *The Practical Sanskrit-English Dictionary*, 1959

Gokhale, B.G., *Buddhism and Asoka*, 1948

Geiger, Wilhelm, *The Mahāvaṁsa*, (tr.), 1912

Hardy, E., *Aśoka*

Hastimalaji Acharya, *Jainadharma Kā Maulika Itihāsa*, I-II, Hindi, 1974

Hultzsch, E., *Corpus Inscriptionum Indicarum*, Vol. I — *Asokan Inscriptions* (2nd edn., 1925)

Hunter, G.R., *The Script of Harappa and Mohenjodaro and its connection with other scripts*

Hunter, W.W., Stirling, A., Beams, J., and Sahu, N.K., *A History of Orissa*, ed. N.K. Sahu, vol. I-II, 1956

Jain, Balchandra, *Kaliṅga Cakravartī*, Hindi, 1954

Jain, Hiralal, *Bhāratīya Saṁsakriti mein Jaina Dharma kā Yogadāna*, Hindi, 1962

Jain, Jyoti Prasad, *Bhāratīya Itihāsa: Eka Dṛṣṭi*, Hindi, 2nd edn., 1966

———, *Pramukha Aitihāsika Jaina Puruṣa aur Mahilāyen*, Hindi, 1974

———, *The Jaina Sources of the History of Ancient India*, 1964

Jain, Nirmal Kumar, *The Cloud-carrier of Kaliṅga* (Meghavāhana Khāravela), fiction, 1982

Jain, Sagarmal, *Sāgara Jaina-Vidyā Bhāratī*, I, 1994

Jayaswal, K.P., *Hindu Polity*

Jina Vijaya, Muni, *Prācīna Jaina Lekha Saṁgraha*, I, 1917

Keith, A.B., *Buddhist Philosophy in India and Ceylon*, 1923

Kern, H., *Manual of Indian Buddhism*, 1896

Kosambi, Dharmanand, *Bhagavān Buddha*, (Hindi trans. Sripad Joshi), 1956

Kuraishi, M.H., *List of Ancient Monuments protected under Act VII of 1904 in the Bihar and Orissa Provinces*, 1938

La Vallée Poussin, L. de, *Bouddhisme Etudes et Materiaux*, 1898

Lamotte, E., *Histoire du Buddhisme Indien*, 1958

Law, B.C., *Historical Geography of Ancient India*, 1954

Lüders, H., *Bruckstucke Buddhistischer Dramen*, 1911

———, *Die Sakischen Mura, BSB*, 1919, pp. 734-66

Mahtab, H.K., *History of Orissa*, Oriya

Majumdar, N.G., *A Guide to the Scluptures in the Indian Museum,* pt. I

Majumdar. S.N., ed., *Ptolemy's Ancient India*

Malalasekara, G.P., *The Pāli Literature of Ceylon*, 1928

Mazumdar, B.C., *Orissa in the Making*

Mehendale, M.A., *Bibliographical Study of Asokan Inscriptions*,

———, *Historical Grammar of Inscriptional Prakrits*, 1948

Minayeff, I.P., *Recherches sur le Bouddhisme*, 1894

Mirashi, V.V., *Sātavāhanon aur Paścimī Kṣatrapon kā Itihāsa aur Abhilekha*, Hindi, 1982

Mitra, Smt. Debala, *Udayagiri and Khaṇḍagiri*, 1959

Mitra, Raja Rajendra Lala, *Antiquities of Orissa*, II, 1880

Mittal, A.C., *An Early History of Orissa*, 1962

Monier-Williams, M., *A Sanskrit-English Dictionary*, 1951

Mookerji, R.K., *Asoka*, 2nd rev. edn., 1955

Nagraj, Muni, *The Contemporaneity and Chronology of Mahāvīra and Buddha*, 1970

Neumann, K.E., *Reden Gotamo Buddhos*, I

Ojha, Gaurishankar Hirachand, *Bhāratīya Prācīna Lipimālā*, Hindi, 1918

Oldenberg, H., *Pātimokkha*, (Trans.), *S.B.E.*, XIII

Oldenberg, H. & Rhys Davids, T.W., *Vinayapiṭakam,* Vol. I, Introduction, 1879

Pandey, Rajbali., *Aśoka ke Dharmalekha*, Hindi, 1957

———, *Indian Palaeagraphy* Pt. I, 2nd edn., 1957

Panigrahi, K.C., *Archaeological Remains at Bhubaneswar*, 1961

Patoria, Kusum, *Yāpanīya aur unkā Sāhitya*, Hindi, 1988

Rai, Suresh Chandra, *Śuṅgarājavaṁśa evaṁ unkā kāla*, Hindi, 1989

Rajguru, S.N., *The Inscriptions of Orissa*, 1959

Ray, N.R., *Maurya and Śuṅga Art,* 1945

Rhys Davids, Mrs., *Sakya or Buddhist Origins*, 1931

Rhys Davds, T.W., *Dialogues of the Buddha*

Sachau, Edward C., *Al-Beruni's India*, II, 1910

Sahu, L.N., *Uḍīsā mein Jaina Dharma*, Hindi tr. Muni Shubhkaran, 1974

Sahu, N.K., *Khāravela*, 1984

Sastri, K.A.N., *A History of South India*, 2nd edn., 1958

Scharfe, H., *The Maurya Dynasty and the Seleucids*, 1971

Schumacher, Wolfgang, *Die Edikte das Kaisers Asoka*, 1948

Senart, E., *Les Inscriptiones de Piyadasi*, 1881

Shah, C.J., *Jainism in North India*, 1931, Hindi translation, 1990

Shah, Umakant P., *Studies in Jaina Art*, 1955

Shamasastry, R., *Kauṭilya's Arthaśāstra*, trans., 4th edn., 1951

Sharma, G.R., *The Excavations at Kauśāmbī*, (1957-59), — *The Defences and the Śyenaciti of the Puruṣamedha*, 1960

Shashi Kant, *Kauśāmbī*, Hindi, 1965

———, *Political and Cultural History of Mid-North India*, 1987

Shastri, Nemichandra, *Tīrthaṅkara Mahāvīra aur unkī Ācārya Paramparā*, I-II, Hindi, 1974

Sircar, D.C., *Select Inscriptions*, Vol. I, 1942, 2nd edn., 1965

Smith, V.A., *Asoka*, *Early History of India*, 4th edn.

———, *Oxford History of India*, 1920

Tarn, W.W., *Greeks in Bactria and India*, 1939, 2nd edn., 1951

Thapar, Romila, *Aśoka and the Decline of the Mauryas*, 1961

Thomas, E.J., *The Life of Buddha*

Tiwary, B.K., *History of Jainism in Bihar*, 1996

Upadhye, A.N., *Pravacanasāra* (*Pavayaṇasāra*), Introduction, 3rd edn., 1964

Upasak, C.S., *The History and Palaeography of Mauryan Brāhmī Script*

Vasantharaj, M.D., *Correlation of the Ages of Bhagavān Mahāveera and Bhagavān Gautama Buddha*, 1997

Vijaymurti, *Jaina Śilālekha Saṁgraha*, II, Hindi, 1952

Walleser, Max, *Das Edict von Bhabra* (*Materalien zur Kunde des Buddhismus*, I, 1923)

———, *Nochmals das Edikt von Bhabra*, *ibid.*, IX, 1925

Winternitz, Maurice, *A History of Indian Literature*, I and II, 2nd edn., 1972

Woolner, A.C., *Aśoka — Text and Glossary*, Pt.I, 1924

———, *Introduction to Prakrit*

III. Journals and Reports, etc.

Acta Orientalia, I, XXXVI (1974) (Copenhagen)

Actes du Sixième Congrès International des Orientalistes, pt. III, sec. 2, 1885

Ancient India (Bulletin of A.S.I.), No. 5 (Jan. 1949)

Anekānta, Hindi, I (1930)

Annals of the Bhandarkar Oriental Research Institute, LIII (1972) (Pune)

Annual Report of the Archaeological Survey of India, 1922-23

Archiv Orientalini, XLII (1974) (Prague)

Asia Major, 5 (1930)

Asiatic Researches, XV

B.C. Law Volume, I

Babu Chhotelal Jain Memorial Volume, 1967

Bhārat Itihās Saṁśodhak Maṇḍaḷ Traimāsik, 52 (1973), Marathi

Bulletin of the School of Oriental and African Studies, 36, 2 (1973) (University of London).

East and West, New Series, XXII, 3-4 (Rome)

Encyclopaedia Jainica — Jaina Viśva-kośa.

Epigraphia Indica, II, VIII, X App., XIII, XX

Grierson Commemoration Volume, 1933

Guru Gopaldas Varaiya Smriti Granth, Hindi, 1967

Indian Antiquary, XX (1891), XXXVI, XL, XLI (1912), XLVII (1918), XLVIII (1919), XLIX (1920).

Indian Archaeology — A Review, 1958-59, 1961-62

Indian Historical Quarterly, II, V, XIV, XXVII

Indian Studies, No. III

Indo-Iranian Journal, XVII, 3-4 (1975) (Leiden)

Jain Hitaishi, Hindi, XV, 5, (March, 1921)

Jain Journal, III, 4

Jaina Antiquary, XIX, 2

Jaina Sandeśa Śodhāṅka, Hindi, VI, VII, XXXI (28-12-1972)

Jaina Siddhānta Bhāskara, Hindi, VI, 1, XV, 2, XVI, 1-2

Journal Asiatique, 1884, 1885, 1887, 1896, 1953

Journal of Andhra Historical Research Society, II

Journal of Bihar and Orissa Research Society, III, IV, VI, XIII, XIV, XV, XVI, XXII, XXIII, XXVIII

Journal of the American Oriental Society, 95.2 (Philadelphia)

Journal of the Asiatic Society of Bengal, VI, IX

Journal of Indian History, XLI, 3

Journal of Oriental Research, XXXVIII (Madras University)

Journal of the Deptt. of Letters, XX (Calcutta University)

Journal of the Pāli Text Society, 1896

Journal of the Rajasthan Institute of Historical Research, IX (1972), (Jaipur)

Journal of the Royal Asiatic Society, 1855 (Vol. 27) 1898, 1901, 1909, 1910, 1911, 1912, 1913, 1915, 1919, 1922, 1963

Journal of the U.P. Historical Society, XX

Mayurbhanj Gazette, IV, 4

Memoirs of the Asiatic Society of Bengal, X

Nāgarī, Hindi, VIII

Parisaṁvāda (4): *Jain Vidyā evaṁ Prakrit* (Sampurnanand Sanskrit University)

Prācī-Jyoti (Digest of Indological Studies), VIII

Prakrit-Vidya, Hindi, April-June, 1999

Proceedings of 2nd All India Oriental Conference, Calcutta, 1922

Purātattva (Bulletin of the Indian Archaeological Society), No. 6 (1972-73)

Quarterly Review of Historical Studies, IX, 4 (1972-73) (Calcutta)

Ṛṣabha Saurabh, 1999

Sacred Books of the East, XIII

Śodhdarśa, Hindi, 36

Svasti Śri (Dr. B.Ch. Chhabra Felicitation Vol.) 1984

The Orissa Historical Resarch Journal, VI, 1

The Oxford School Atlas, 29th edn., 1997

Tulsī Prajñā, XVIII, 4 (28-2-1993)

University of Ceylon Review, XVIII (1960)

Vishveshvarananda Indological Journal, V, X (Hoshiarpur)

Index